CW01430551

The Tides of Love and War

War brought them together, before tearing them apart with little hope of reunion

By

Kevin Parker

Copyright © 2024 by – Kevin Parker – All Rights Reserved.

It is not legal to reproduce, duplicate, or transmit any part of this document in either electronic means or printed format. Recording of this publication is strictly prohibited.

i

'For there is nothing either good or bad, but thinking makes it so'

Hamlet Act 2 – William Shakespeare

This is a story about how war first brought two people together in a way that would have never happened otherwise, and then kept them apart with a will that almost seemed planned. It reflects how war mixes people, rich and poor, city dwellers and country dwellers, and from all sorts of different locations.

The two main characters, with good intent, are wafted along by the incessant currents of war. It's also how those involved on all sides of the struggle, sometimes conduct themselves in less favourable ways. It can be easy though in times of war to judge people as good or bad, but many people do wonderful things in extremely adverse situations and others succumb to acts of cruelty with little provocation.

If there is a villain in this story then it is war itself. I hope that as you read this story, and learn more about the absurdities and awfulness of wartime, you might also read it with Hamlet's words in mind

Contents

About the Author vi

World War Two - Timeline of Events 1

Chapter 1. Anzio, March 1944 7

Chapter 2. Suffolk May 1944 21

Chapter 3. Shropshire June 1942................................ 34

Chapter 4. London & Belfast 1943............................... 56

Chapter 5. Stalag VIIIC 70

Chapter 6. The Land Army 92

Chapter 7. The Long March 107

Chapter 8. WLA In Wales 1943-4 125

Chapter 9. Liberation & Escape 1944 136

Chapter 10.   June 1945 158

Chapter 11.   Cardiff 1945 175

For my Mum & Dad

My Family for support and information

About the Author

Kevin was born and raised in Cardiff and is a proud Welshman.

He had a successful career in driving organisational change and building leadership capability.

This is his first novel, although he has published a business book in the past and he has been listed in Britain 'Who's Who'.

He is a passionate sailor and a fully qualified yacht master.

He lives in Herefordshire, looking down over the river Wye. He is married with two grown-up children, three grown up step children and three grandchildren.

World War Two - Timeline of Events

1939

Aug 31	-Civilian evacuations begin from London.
Sept 1	-Nazis invade Poland.
Sept 3	-Britain & France declare war on Germany.

1940

Jan 8	-Rationing begins in Britain.
April 9	-Nazis invade Denmark and Norway.
May 10	-Nazis invade France, Belgium, and the Netherlands
May 10	-Winston Churchill becomes British Prime Minister.
May 26	-Evacuation of Allied troops from Dunkirk begins.
June 3	-Dunkirk evacuation ends.
June 10	-Italy declares war on Britain and France.
June 22	-France signs an armistice with Nazi Germany.
July 1 Atlantic.	-German U-boats attack merchant ships in the
Aug 15	-Air battles and daylight raids over Britain.
Aug 17	-Hitler declares a blockade of the British Isles.
Aug 25	-First British air raid on Berlin.
Sept 3	-Hitler plans the invasion of Britain
Sept 7	-German Blitz against Britain begins.

Sept 13	-Italians invade Egypt.
Sept 15	-Massive German air raids on British Cities
Sept 27	-Axis Pact signed by Germany, Italy and Japan.
Oct 31	-Battle of Britain ends
Dec 9 Italians.	-British begin offensive in North Africa against the
Dec 29	-Massive German air raid on London.

1941

Jan 22 Australians.	-Tobruk in North Africa falls to the British and
Feb 14 Africa.	-First units of German 'Afrika Korps' arrive in North
May 10/11 Hamburg.	-Heavy German bombing of London; British bomb
May 27	-Sinking of the Bismarck by the British Navy.
June 22	-Germany attacks Soviet Union
Aug 20	-Nazi siege of Leningrad begins.
Dec 5	-German attack on Moscow is abandoned.
Dec 7	-Japanese bomb Pearl Harbour
Dec 8	-United States and Britain declare war on Japan.
Dec 11	-Hitler declares war on the United States.

1942

Jan 26	-First American forces arrive in Great Britain.

April 23   -German air raids begin against cathedral cities in
Britain.

May 30   -First thousand-bomber British air raid (against
Cologne).

June   -Mass murder of Jews by gassing begins at
Auschwitz.

June 21   -Rommel captures Tobruk.

July 22   -Treblinka extermination camp opened.

Sept 13   -Battle of Stalingrad begins.

Nov 1   -Allies break Axis lines at El Alamein

Nov 8   -Allied Invasion of N Africa

Dec 17   -Anthony Eden tells House of Commons of mass
executions of Jews

1943

Feb 2   -Germans surrender at Stalingrad in the first big
defeat of Hitler's armies.

Mar 16-20   -Battle of Atlantic climaxes with 27 merchant ships
sunk by German U-boats.

May 13   -German and Italian troops surrender in North
Africa.

May 22   -Dönitz suspends U-boat operations in the North
Atlantic.

July 9/10   -Allies land in Sicily.

Sept 8   -Italian surrender to Allies is announced.

Sept 9   -Allied landings on Italian mainland.

Sept 11	-Germans occupy Rome.
Oct 1	-Allies enter Naples.
Oct 13	-Italy declares war on Germany
Nov	-Large British air raid on Berlin.

1944

Jan 6	-Soviet troops advance into Poland.
Jan 22	-Allies land at Anzio in Italy.
Jan 27	-Leningrad relieved after a 900-day siege.
Feb 16	-Germans counter-attack against the Anzio beachhead.
May 25	-Germans retreat from Anzio.
June 5	-Allies enter Rome.
June 6	-D-Day landings take place on the northern coast of France.
June 13	- First German V-1 rocket attack on Britain.
Aug 25	-Paris Liberated
Dec 16-27	-Battle of the Bulge fought in the Ardennes.

1945

Jan 26	-Soviet troops liberate Auschwitz.
Feb 13/14	-Dresden is destroyed by a firestorm after allied bombing raids.

27 Mar-Last V2 rocket lands in London

April 12	-Allies liberate Buchenwald and Belsen concentration camps

April 16	-Soviet troops begin their final attack on Berlin
April 30	-Adolf Hitler commits suicide.
May 7	-German forces unconditionally surrender all to Allies.
May 8	-V-E (Victory in Europe) Day.

The Tides of Time

Time is a tricky concept by which to live
And scientists tell us that it's all relative.
So, how can time be truly measured?
Since our span of it is really treasured.

Simple counting has too many limits
The years, months, days, and minutes,
In many ways, just do not show,
How time passes fast, and then so slow

Tides provide more descriptive modes
With their floods and slack, and ebb and flows,
Regular ever-changing cycles we can predict
Following our moons never changing orbit

High tides bring unexpected treasures
As good times bring us many pleasures
Low tides reveal many hidden secrets
As bad times may bring us sad regrets

Tidal floods take all before them
Before slack water restores decorum
It has its own relentless force,
As we need to stop. And sometimes pause

Surprising, what tides may bring our way
And what they will then just take away
What's certain is life's short span
And time and tide wait for no man

Chapter 1.   Anzio, March 1944

After an uneasy and frustrating peace during the first two weeks after the landing, the battle of Anzio began in earnest in February. The Allied forces tried to break out for several months, and losses were heavy.

Behind the Anzio beaches, the wide marshy land had been ravaged by the incessant bombardment by the Germans. This had been compounded by the flooding of the marshes with seawater, both intentionally by the Germans and as a result of their bombardment. The marshes now stank with salty stagnant water, which would gradually turn into a melting pot for disease should the Allied forces not break out soon.

This was not proving easy due to their puzzling early inactivity after the initial landing, which had seemed to allow the Axis forces to regroup, reinforce, and surround the Allies.

It was an eerily quiet February day on the marshy insect-ridden marches inland from the sandy beaches of Anzio. Even the humble but ethereal skylarks, with their melodic song were enjoying the peace, hovering in the air above them, hoping to collect insects rising during the marginally warmer mid-afternoon. With great effort, this bird sang continuously while zooming up into the air, holding steady aloft and then plummeting down. An exultation of skylarks was their collective name, and it was easy to see why.

Sam watched them with twin emotions. He enjoyed being a spectator of one of nature's joys, and they reminded him of his Shropshire country upbringing and his home. He particularly missed his country walks with Christine. He loved her warmth and chatter and how she had grown to love the countryside as much as he did. He couldn't help wondering and worrying about how she was dealing with the worries about her parents still in London and living through the German bombing raids.

He had met Christine eight months before leaving for his military service in North Africa, en-route to Sicily and now here in Italy. In their relatively short time together, they had become very close. He prayed they would someday be able to return to continue their promising relationship. He had written to her as often as he could but had little idea whether she had received all his letters. He knew they were heavily redacted so as not to give anything away to the Germans, and it was hard to write anything very meaningful. He had only received two replies. He kept them on him all the time and read and re-read repeatedly, and now had to handle them very carefully as we're getting increasingly fragile and dog-eared with the use. He gently opened her last letter and read it through once more.

My Darling Sam,

It's so strange and worrying knowing that you are on some distant shore facing such imminent danger. I'm really quite glad your war is proving boring so far, because at least that means you are safe, and that's what I want more than anything. It is difficult to imagine what life is like for you. Please tell me what you can when you can.

I have now properly joined the WLA, and I'm working at a farm in the middle of nowhere in Suffolk. The farmer and his wife are not that friendly, and the conditions are pretty basic. I've learned a lot about farming, though and you would be proud of me, I'm sure. I can milk a cow, feed the bullocks and even drive a tractor. I feel at last that I'm doing something for the war effort.

At least there are a few other WLA girls here, and we get on well. On Saturdays, there is quite a good dance at the local village, and you would be amazed at what the Yanks get up to on the dance floor, especially the black GI's. Their dancing and music are amazing. You are such a good dancer Sam, you would love it too if only, only, you could be here.

My Mum and Dad are well, and the blitz seems to be coming to an end, thank god. I do worry about them so much, and now there is the threat of these self-propelled doodlebug bombs. You can hear them coming, making a terrible tearing and rasping sound, and then there is a dreadful silence before you hear the explosion. When they explode, they create a whip-cracking sound, and then very soon after this comes the chaos of the explosion with debris and earth churned skyward. There is no warning. It's s so frightening and there is nothing you can do but pray. At least there aren't as many of them as there were in the blitz

Can't fit much more on here. Let's hope this terrible war is over soon. You keep away from those Germans as much as you can. I want you in one piece - do you hear! I look at the stars every night, and I think I know which one Beetlejuice is now, and I think of you

With all my love - Christine xxxxx

His thoughts of her and the knowledge that she was relatively safe had sustained him during the seemingly never-ending campaign so far. Although Christine was from London, which was being regularly bombed - he had visited her parents there - he was so glad she was now in the safety of the Suffolk countryside. The war had brought them together in a way that would normally have been very improbable. Now it was doing its very best to do the opposite, it seemed, in keeping them apart.

Sam was about average height, five foot nine inches tall, with a shock of black hair. He was a stocky build and weighed in at just under twelve stone. He had not been particularly involved in sport when he was young, but the country lifestyle and all the cycling that he did had always kept him in reasonable physical shape. He was now, of course, even fitter than he had ever been as a result of his recent army training.

Before the war, he had been destined to have an ordinary and fairly quiet life. He was a bright lad and might well have gone to grammar school if his parents could have afforded it. Instead, he was due to start an apprenticeship in a small tractor repair business. His Dad was a farrier as was his dad before him. In fact, the family name, Blackstone, could be found on local church gravestones reaching back for centuries past, and he was always proud to mention that it was in the Doomsday book. 'We come from a long line of peasants ', his father would say with a smile.

He had had a secure country boy upbringing, filling his days with a mixture of boyhood adventures and pranks and helping with the chores. Bethan, his sister, the youngest of eight, was his closest sibling, and there was a five-year age gap between them and the next oldest, his sister Mary. His older brothers were in reserved occupations, and he was the only one of his family to be in the army.

A fear of open water was the only real personality quirk he had developed in his youth, and he steadfastly refused to learn to swim. This fear was the result of a childhood accident when he was seven. Playing by himself on the ice of the local pond that January, it cracked and gave way, and despite struggling hard, he fell into the freezing water. The shock was frightening, and being clothed was dragging him down. This might have seen the end of him, as there was no one around to hear his frantic cries. He panicked, splashing around desperately and very nearly drowned as a result. Luckily while flailing around, he just managed to grab a branch, and used this to struggle out. Exhausted, cold and very shaken, he made his own shivering, shuffling walk home. The experience frightened him badly, and he avoided water and any encouragement to swim thereafter. It was ironic, therefore, that his first few experiences of action in the army involved landings from the sea.

His first landing had been in North Africa followed by landings in Sicily and now Anzio. Luckily, at each of these, he had not come under much fire so far, and he had seen little action. The landing at Anzio had not been without incident, though. Two soldiers in his group fell into the sea while getting onto to launches. Because they were carrying all their gear, they sank very quickly, and no one was able to save them. This was shocking on its own, but obviously also did little to allay his fears

After this quiet landing, they moved a little inland and made camp. They then spent weeks not far from the landings wondering what their next orders would be, frustrated at not doing anything while pleased that at least they had not come under fire. But now, after endless weeks of doing very little, his division had been given their

11

orders to advance. They were to head east over unhealthy bog land, part of the notorious Pontine Marshes. Large areas had been reclaimed, and farming settlements had been formed. One of these was known as Aprilia and was on the main road about nine miles north of Anzio. By common consent the settlement buildings became known as the 'Factory,' They had been built by Mussolini in a supposedly modern style so that although they were houses, they apparently looked like a large factory, they were told. That was their next destination.

The marshes were criss-crossed by numerous canals and irrigation channels and deep wadis which, when the rains fell as they had, became quickly flooded. Some of the wadis were fifty feet deep with sheer sides.

As they set off, and apart from the noise of marching men, everything was very quiet. They were anxious at first but after an hour of expecting the worst, they settled down to walking through and around marshy ground and focusing on not slipping up. His sergeant, during training, had told them that soldiering was ninety per cent boredom and ten per cent absolute terror. So far, it had been mostly boredom, and he was more than happy for it to continue that way.

After about an hour, the quietness gave way to the feeling of an unreal naturalness. Their world was suddenly, shockingly, shattered by enemy rifle and machine gun fire from somewhere ahead of them as their platoon came under fire for the first time. Now, also for the first time, Sam had to fire his gun in anger at an enemy soldier. It shocked him to the core. He wasn't exactly sure where to aim, along with quite a few of his comrades.

"Point your bloody guns at the enemy and fire", bellowed the sergeant, who had obviously noticed the confusion. The sergeant's shout broke Sam out of his shocked haze, and he did what was ordered. Some of his comrades around him were soon receiving gunshot injuries, and it dawned upon him that he must be causing some of this carnage to the German soldiers he was firing at. This was bearable if awful in itself, but what followed next was not only going to be harrowing but also life-changing.

Emerging unexpectedly from the ditch, no more than twenty yards away from him, appeared a tall, young-ish German soldier. They both froze at this unexpected turn of events, and just stared at each other, knowing what they were supposed to do next, but neither being willing to do it. Sam could see the fear in the other's eyes, which reflected the fear in him, and his hands were starting to shake and sweat. They both knew that they had to do something, but what? Should he surrender to him, run away or fire at him? This short moment seemed to last and last until, suddenly, a rifle shot nearby startled them into action, and they both moved slightly, breaking the silent impasse. Thinking the German was starting to attack him, he raised his rifle and started to move, and the German did the same. Once this momentum started, it was like a dam had burst, and they ran at each other, firing wildly and yelling in some visceral, basic bestial way. He neither thought nor cared about his opponent as shots screamed past him. A red mist descended on him. There was no rational thought anymore; this was purely about living or dying. His basic raw survival instinct had kicked in.

The German dodged to his left but, in doing so, lost his footing, tripped and fell awkwardly, obviously breaking or twisting something that was making it difficult for him to get up. He was still firing wildly, though. Sam knew he still was a danger to himself and everyone else if he wasn't stopped. Sam obviously now had the advantage in manoeuvrability and knew he could better him. He fired and dodged and fired again, and one of his shots obviously hit its mark as the German screamed in pain and stopped firing. Suddenly, Sam was there, standing over him. He was shaking with the battle rage that had engulfed him like a wild, unwanted stranger urging him to finish the job.

"Nein, Nein," wailed the German in desperation but still pointing his rifle at him. The German had grabbed a photo from his pocket that pictured a woman and two young children and waved it at him with tears in his eyes. He pointed at the photo and shouted in fear, "Mein Sohn und meine Frau!"

Sam hesitated, and the rage reduced its grip on his senses. For the first time in this encounter, he saw him as a man and not some anonymous enemy trying to kill him or be killed. But the German had still not lowered his gun. He hesitated, thinking for an instant what to do.

In that moment of hesitation, a grenade burst with ear shattering noise nearby. The shrapnel flew around them like angry stinging wasps. Instinctively he dived to the ground. When he looked up again, his ears still ringing from the noise of the blast, the German soldier was lying dead. The top half of his head was now missing, but he was still holding the photo tightly in his now lifeless hand. Sam felt the violent urge to be sick at the sight and turned and retched repeatedly where he stood. He stayed there, frozen to the spot but still trembling with the overdose of adrenaline. Shouting around him suddenly brought him to his senses. The men from his platoon were calling to him, "This way now! Run, run for it. We are outnumbered and have to regroup!"

Sam ran off to join the others. In the confused retreat that followed, Sam and a group of about fifty men somehow became separated from the rest of their company. After eventually regrouping, they could not see the others in their Company, but they knew they just had to move on. Hoping that they were moving in the right direction, they headed off, keeping as close as they had to, towards the stinking, insect-filled ditches for some degree of cover. They had little alternative anyway.

After a while, they reorganised themselves into some semblance of order. In a line of about fifty, they now advanced carefully across a flat, slightly higher, and so more easily traversed, area of land. They were walking a line abreast, spread out across the ground about twenty feet apart, walking slowly but purposely forward. They walked cautiously and carefully with their Lee Enfield Rifles again held ready for action. After the previous burst of action, calmness and an eerie silence now reigned.

Sam still felt very badly shaken. He had always hoped he would never knowingly see that he had killed someone. While he still hadn't as far as he knew yet, he knew if it wasn't for that grenade, in that paroxysm of rage in that moment, he might well have. He at least now was able to regain some of his composure as a result of this slow, uneventful progress over the following twenty minutes. War was portrayed in terms of fighting an enemy for a good cause. When it came down to it, though, he thought it was simply a disgusting business of killing just an ordinary man with an ordinary family who just happened to have been born in a different place. Since that moment, a moment that would be forever etched in his memory, the reality had hit him like a sickening punch to his guts. Other soldiers had said to him in the past that the first time was always the worst. He didn't ever want there to be a second time, but he knew there would probably have to be. He hated that thought.

He was now positioned towards the left side of this line. The badge of the Royal London Irish Rifles, a famous Northern Ireland regiment, was showing proudly on the front of his khaki uniform.

How he had been enlisted into an Ulster regiment was unusual in itself, as Sam was born, raised, and then signed up in Shropshire, but such were the vagaries, essentials and sometimes randomness of events in wartime. He had undergone his training in Omagh, Northern Ireland, southeast of Belfast. The natives were very friendly and welcoming people and made him feel at home very quickly. After an initial six-week training, he was billeted for a time with a family there. He had become firm friends with Fergus their son, who was also in his Company and who was now walking to his left.

Fergus had a strong Ulster accent that Sam often teased him about. He was different to Sam in many ways, tall and wiry with a shock of ginger hair and a buoyant sense of humour that had seen them through many tough days so far. He enjoyed the 'craic' as Fergus called it. They shared the same sense of humour, and both had similar country backgrounds.

Deafening thunderous explosions from nowhere once more shattered the peace. This time, it was the enemy artillery breaking loose. The sound was a deafening cacophony. The air was at once chaotically full of churning earth, debris and the acrid stench of explosives. The screaming shells exploded all around them, throwing their shrapnel around like a storm full of steel shards. Any moment, Sam felt he was about to be hit, and men around him started to run, in more panic than any sort of order, as fast as they could towards a ditch that they could make out a few hundred yards ahead, hoping it would provide at least some hope of refuge. For those few moments at least, their training went out of the window, and the raw sense of self-survival took over.

The artillery fire was deadly accurate, though, finding its victims, and soon, men started to fall around him. He could hear cries and screams from all directions as men were thrown down and broken by the exploding shells and shrapnel. He looked across to his friend Fergus, who shouted or rather mouthed across to him, as it was almost impossible to hear anything apart from the gunfire "All right, mucker?"

Sam was in the process of trying to mouth a reply to his friend, but at that very moment, a shell exploded over Fergus, and he simply disappeared in the explosion. Sam was thrown over by the blast, but as he regained his composure, he looked himself over and realised he at least was uninjured. To his disgust and horror, he had felt something splatter over him as he was blown over. He now realised it was human remains. And not anyone's remains, but what must have been some of his dead friends. With no time to think on this, his survival instinct kicked in again, and in a state of numbed shock he just stumbled onwards through the chaos and finally made the ditch. The ditch offered little in the way of safety, and the survivors looked around for a safer refuge.

Just past the ditch was a ruined outbuilding, and so the remnants of the group managed to scramble, crawl, and scrabble their way to the hopeful shelter of these ruins. Eventually, just eight survived the chaos and flung themselves into this shelter. They sat together in this temporary but relative safety, they thought at least. Catching their breath, they sat and gazed at each other in shocked disbelief.

Basic training had never prepared them for this. It was the first experience of action for most of them.

Sam seemed to be the first one to regain some composure and asked, "How is everyone? Is anyone injured?"

None of the remaining eight seemed to have any major injuries apart from minor burns, gashes and bruises. No one of any rank had survived, though, and they felt leaderless, lost and scared.

Outside, the shelling carried on for a short while, but at least it appeared not to be aimed at them anymore. Then, it stopped almost as abruptly as it started, leaving a silence as loud as the shelling. While the gunfire was terrifying, the silence started to prove more so. They sat in a stunned, shocked silence, wondering what to do. Sam no longer thought of home or the future, he wanted to get out of there and just survive this hell. As he sat there, he thought of his friend Fergus and couldn't believe that this warm, friendly happy man was no more. He vowed to visit his family if he survived and at least write to them as soon as he could. He was going to miss him hugely. So, this is what war really is, he thought, no glamour or excitement, just terror and loss

By now, it was late afternoon, and it would soon be starting to get dark. They started to discuss what to do next.

One soldier said, "I think we should just rest and hide."

Another said, "We should surrender; we can't fight our way out." And another: We can't stay here."

They seemed to be looking to Sam for answers. While he had no seniority over them, he had noticed in training that he had become something of an informal leader.

Sam said, "Look, we don't know what's happening out there and what we should do next. We should take a cautious look outside to see what's happening."

As he was nearest the door, he volunteered. He cautiously emerged, looking carefully around him. He suddenly froze, dropped his rifle, and then shouted, waving his arms frantically. The reason for this apparently strange reaction was the appearance of a burly German soldier about twenty yards away in the act of throwing a grenade towards their refuge.

"Nein, nein," he shouted in the only German he knew.

The soldier saw him and, with the sudden realisation that this fighting was over, instead, thankfully and amazingly, threw the grenade to deliberately miss their refuge. It exploded loudly but harmlessly on the other side of the ruined building. Turning his head, he shouted something in German, and at least twenty of his comrades emerged from the ditch behind him. They walked towards Sam, guns raised, shouting repeatedly,

"Achtung! Auslieferung!"

Sam didn't understand their words but didn't need to as their meaning was clear enough. He was in no mood to think of resisting and quickly raised his arms and then shouted to the others.

"We have to surrender. We are outnumbered. Come on out slowly and throw down your guns so that they know we are surrendering."

They offered no resistance and followed Sam's advice. His fighting war appeared to be over. Given his experiences that day, that was somewhat of a relief in many ways. However now facing a very uncertain and worrying future, he realised sadly that his chances of getting home anytime soon were fast fading away.

The German troops soon rounded them up and roughly checked them for any other weapons. They were efficient and reasonably calm, and although they shouted at them and ordered them around, they were not violent and didn't seem to be a threat in any way.

They were organised into a short column with only four guards. Not that that mattered, as none of them were in the mood to challenge their guards. He was tired and hungry and just wanted a quiet place to rest and eat. As he was led away with the others, he reflected on the way he had reacted to the face-to-face life-and-death situations he had experienced in the last few hours, how he had dealt with them, and how his now captor who had held the grenade, had made an instant decision to save life and not end it aimlessly. Who was the real enemy, he thought.

Chapter 2. Suffolk May 1944

In all, 3.5 million children lived through the cataclysmic experience of evacuation during the Second World War. Some were away for a few weeks; others were separated from their families for up to six years. Homecoming was not always easy, and a few described it as harder than going away in the first place.

The blitz in London started in early September 1940. It lasted every night for almost a month before tailing off into more sporadic raids but just as terrorising. Falling shells from anti-aircraft guns killed as many as bombing. The main impact was less than anticipated in terms of casualties but far more in general disruption and the impact on housing.

Although initially, the bombing did enormous damage to the docklands, it was only when it spread out to the whole of London that the damage it did was hugely outweighed by the positive impact it had on the resolve of the British people. Somehow, people just carried on with their ordinary lives.

At its height one hundred and seventy thousand people sheltered in the underground stations overnight. Trains acted as mobile food distributors to feed them.

The day had started out like any other ordinary day, even though they were living in extraordinary times.

The May sky was a uniform grey, and Suffolk's flat landscape seemed to magnify this miserable greyness. The sky seemed to stretch on forever, with little in this flat land to disrupt the horizon. The fields, in contrast, however, were full of life and colour. Early summer brought an overabundance. It was as if all plants were chaotically competing with each other, trying to get the maximum out of the warmer weather before the changing seasons forced them to retire gracefully.

The fields had been planted mainly with cereal crops that were almost ready to harvest. One very large field was full of barley and nearing its time to be harvested. The weeds were competing single-mindedly with the crops to have their day in the sun, and it was hard work holding them back to ensure the barley won and delivered a good harvest, which was, of course, vital for the war effort.

What might have been a tranquil scene was being rudely ruptured by the monotonous mechanical throbbing sound of aircraft circling overhead like giant, noisy vultures. The American B17 bombers needed, after taking off from the nearby US base, to circle around overhead for a time after take-off, in order to organise themselves into their neat and mutually protective bombing formations. The faint smell of fumes and gasoline from these sinister machines lingered in the air and, for a while, at least diminished the otherwise much fresher country smells of the crops, the newly turned earth, and the wildflowers.

Three young women were working in the field, hoeing the weeds between the barley stalks and only occasionally looking up at the aerial display overhead. They had become used to what was an almost daily flying routine that was only ever interrupted when bad weather made it difficult to fly. The girls were all slim and rosy-cheeked from the hard physical outdoor work and were all dressed in their standard land army clothing, consisting of boots, woollen calf-length socks, brown corduroy breeches, a fawn shirt and green v-neck wool jumpers.

Plodding slowly across the nearby field in their general direction was an obviously different, older and more corpulent figure. She was wearing a headscarf, an old well-worn, home-knitted grey jumper, and an ill-fitting and unflattering pair of blue dungarees tucked into her Wellington boots. She was the rather unfriendly farmer's wife, Mrs Piper. The girls took little notice of her even though it was unusual to see her stray away from the farmyard. She was usually too busy with the myriad of other farm chores to have time to visit the fields, and besides, the girls were carrying out pretty routine tasks that needed little checking anyway.

One of the Land Girls, Christine, stopped hoeing, wiped her hand gently across her brow and looked up a little longer at the planes silhouetted in the sky above. She was only eighteen but felt like she had already had a lifetime of experiences. Her thoughts were drawn towards what might be the bombers' destination somewhere, she guessed, in Germany. They precipitated thoughts about her boyfriend, Sam. They had had only a short time together before he set sail for North Africa but their relationship had developed and blossomed quickly. Sam had been part of the Allied invasion force somewhere in the North Mediterranean. His last letter to her told her that he was to be part of what she now knew to be the Anzio landings. Letters had to be brief and fit a standard-sized sheet. Everyone had learned to write as small as possible and be careful not to give any information away. Anything too specific was blacked out.

My Darling Christine,

We have been told we are on our way from Sicily tomorrow heading for somewhere in Italy to somehow relieve the army at somewhere called Monte Casino.

Although I'm not looking forward to another sea journey, it will be good to move on. Army life can be very monotonous, and if it wasn't for my mates hear, especially Fergus, it would be very boring. He's a great character, full of fun, and I hope you will be able to meet him someday when this is all over.

North Africa is very strange, very dry, and little vegetation where we are, and it's so hot. The locals seem to be doing very good business selling their version of tea and quite bitter but refreshing lemon juice. I don't ask where they get their water from, and it's nowhere obvious.

Anyway, my love, how are you? Have you started in the Land Army yet? I hope you are not in London anymore as we hear the bombing continues. Don't worry about me. I can see me going through this war never having fired a shot if things continue for me as they have

Wish I could write more. I miss you and think of you always. Remember Beetlejuice. All my love, Sam xxxxx

The latest news, however, from Italy was not good, as the Allied forces had seemingly made little progress for over a month. Fighting, she gathered from the news was hard with strong resistance from the German forces that had had time to regroup. She had not heard from him since that letter before the landings.

The physical and repetitive farm work gave her little time for reflection, and, at least as a result, this gave Christine some relief from her worries about him and also her parents, who were living in London. Their house had mercifully survived the blitz but was then destroyed by a V1 flying bomb very shortly afterwards. They, though, had luckily survived because, amazingly, they had not been home when it happened. They were ok and were now having to live with relatives. Although the terror of the blitz was over, they now faced this new and constant torment from these unseen and unpredictable flying bombs or doodlebugs as they had become known.

Christine was just over five foot one, had reddish blonde curly hair, blue-grey eyes, a ready smile and laugh, which could often easily dissolve into a fit of the giggles, especially when her sister joined in. Brought up in North London in a lower middle-class family, her early childhood had been idyllic. She was very close to Elsie, her elder sister, by two years and was surrounded by a warm and happy extended family. Her dad was a shoemaker for the famous Lilley and Skinners in Southwark, and her mum was a housewife. She remembered visits to the zoo, walks around Hampstead Heath and sitting near there in the gardens of the Old Bull and Bush, visits to relatives in Chippenham and trips to the seaside. This almost idyllic initial childhood had grounded her in strong family values of kindness, support and mutual respect, together with a sense of fun and easy laughter

25

Nothing in her early life prepared her, or indeed few others, for what was to come when war broke out. She had been healthy and worry-free until she had a serious bout of scarlet fever, which was then a dangerously contagious illness when she was seven. She was taken to Brook General Hospital at Shooters Hill, Woolwich and put in a ward with about 20 other children. Delirious and semi-conscious, much of the time, ice was packed on her to try and get her high temperature down, and nurses bathed her in pungent-smelling disinfectant. Visitors were not allowed inside the ward. Her only communication with family and friends was through a closed exterior window from the grounds as they filed past along the long, covered veranda there. She was detained there for a full five months until it was felt safe to discharge her back into her family.

While this experience had only left her with a slight physical defect, now being a little deaf in her left ear, it had left a more significant legacy on her personality. She had become more reserved, and it didn't take much to start her worrying about anything. The fact that she had survived this experience, however, in a strange way, had also helped her develop an inner resilience and reliance on her own resources. This was to serve her well in the years to come. It also had an impact on her education as she found it difficult to catch up almost half a school year. She was never an academic, though, and it was her strengths in building relationships with all ages that helped her and would help her through stressful times in her future.

When the war broke out in 1939, her safe, secure family existence was to change dramatically. She was fourteen and was evacuated to Luton with many other children from London.

She left Euston Station with many other children. Her mum was obviously very emotional but put on a brave face seeing her off. Christine felt she would have to do the same, although inside, her stomach was churning, and she wanted to stay with all her heart. Much as she didn't want to leave, she was determined not to cry. She knew her mum was upset, and she didn't want to make it worse for both of them.

As the train moved off, she waved to her mum and choked back the tears. It all seemed to be unreal to begin with, and she couldn't believe she wouldn't be home again soon. After leaving London's suburbs, the train chugged through the countryside until, after about an hour's train journey, the train pulled into Luton station. She and the other children were then walked across town, many of them sobbing still. As one of the older ones she felt it her duty to try and comfort some of them. They all ended up late that afternoon in a hall in Luton with many other children from many other schools. She knew some of the other children from her school, but they had deliberately split up class groups. Christine sat there miserably with the others. Nobody talked much, and the unusual quietness was broken down from time to time by someone sobbing.

A middle-aged stern looking woman with a clipboard clutched firmly in her hand called everyone to attention.

"Now, children, you are all to be billeted with families during the course of the day. Local families will arrive over the next few hours, and you will be selected to go with them when it's your turn. So, I want you all to behave and look your best."

Families willing to take children filtered in during the day looked around and then made their choices. One by one, the numbers dwindled, and many of her friends departed. Christine was never picked. It seemed that no one wanted an older child, especially a girl, and she felt very lonely and miserable.

At the end of the day, feeling very tired and very unwanted, she was then virtually dragged through the streets with a small group of others who had also not been housed yet, whilst the largely unsympathetic billeting officers, intent on housing everyone before night-time, knocked on doors, asking people to take a child in. She was almost the last to be billeted. She felt really unwelcome. The family, who were eventually virtually forced to take her, did so with great reluctance.

They obviously resented having to take her in, and she already hated it there. Her new 'foster parents,' Mr and Mrs Bulpin, told her plainly that they did not want her there and she had been forced on them. Mrs Bulpin treated her almost slave-like, showing no affection at all. Christine felt she hated her.

The next morning, she had to see herself off to school in the morning. Mrs Bulpin said that she wasn't to be allowed in the house if Mrs Bulpin was out when she returned home.

Over time, things got worse and worse. She would be sent out in the bitterly cold weather to run errands and do bits of shopping. Her hands became chilblained, and she always felt hungry. She was often sent into the scullery to eat just one slice of bread and lard for her evening meal because she had supposedly misbehaved in some way she didn't understand. Although she never told her parents the details about how she was treated, she wrote letter after letter to them, begging them to let her come home.

Her real Mum visited every month even though the authorities tried to persuade them not to as they thought this wasn't good for parents and children. Special coaches were laid on for these visits, though. Her Mum told her she had sent her money and parcels but she never saw them and didn't like to tell her mum she hadn't either, and so lied to her about having received them. She hid her emotions so her mum wouldn't worry, but both shed a tear when they departed.

Much as her mum and Christine would like to be together, there was serious pressure on her and all parents not to let their children return home. On the way to school one day, she saw a sinister poster issued by the Ministry of Health, which featured a mother sitting beside a tree in the country with a town in the distance. Frolicking before her were two little boys, and behind her, in ghostly outline, was Hitler whispering, 'Take them back!' The mother looked anxious. The caption read: 'Don't do it, Mother. Leave the children where they are.' The implication was obvious; her mother would be regarded as a traitor if she ignored official advice and brought her home. She cried when she saw it and wanted to cover it up if she could. Nevertheless, Christine kept up the stream of letters to her parents asking to come home.

There had been a period of false peace, and the promised bombing of London by Hitler had not yet started. She was now almost fifteen too, and so, eventually, after eight months, her parents gave in and allowed her back in early June 1940. She was so pleased to be home and vowed she would never complain about anything to them ever again.

Despite the increasing German threat and the reverses on the battlefield in mainland Europe, culminating in the humiliating evacuation from Dunkirk, nothing really happened in London until early September that year. An uneasy, nervous peace settled over London. Everyone knew it couldn't last, but everyone wanted it to.

Saturday 7th September 1940 was not a special day normally, but it was a beautiful sunny day. London went about its usual business in glorious sunshine. It was still hard to believe for most people that there was a war going on. People got on with their lives.

Christine was on her way home from college where she was training to be a nanny, and didn't notice anything different. At four pm, however, she noticed at first just a few people stopped. And then they stared at the sky. She stopped and looked up, too, and very soon, it seemed the whole city stopped and stared towards the sky. A massive armada of what people soon started to realise were German planes heading up the River Thames, like a black, threatening, sinister shadow. It was difficult to count the numbers, but later estimates in the newspapers said that over three hundred bombers and over six hundred fighters blotted out the sky.

Christine ran home, her stomach churning with fright. Her parents were just emerging to find out what the commotion was outside. She, along with her parents and the rest of the people on their road, rushed down to the end of the road, where there was a better view over London, to see what was going on and looked up to see this startling spectacle in the sky. Suddenly, the anti-aircraft guns woke and started opening up, and they could see the explosions amongst the German formations appearing suddenly like puffs of cloud followed later by the dull thuds of the explosions. She thought she could just make out British fighter planes that were weaving in and out of the German formations. It was to those watching from a distance, quite a show, and there was a buzz as everybody talked about what they were seeing with a mixture of fear and excitement. That night, however, when she looked out of her bedroom window, she could see the docklands glowing red, and this brought home some of the reality of what had happened. She continued to hear the thud, thud, thud of bombers delivering their deathly damage well until the early hours of the morning.

The raids, once started, continued day after day after day, with no let-up. For a while, apart from reading of the devastation in the papers, this daily show didn't affect most Londoners living away from the docklands. Then, after a week, the terror spread to other parts of London, and soon Christine and her family began to spend most nights in their shelter. Most nights, the sirens would wail their eerie warning sound, and they would move with bedding and provisions into their Anderson shelter in the back garden. This was no more than a galvanised curved corrugated steel plate dug into the ground and covered with earth. Her Dad had constructed this from parts and plans delivered to every house. Despite her Mum and Dad's best efforts to make it homely, it was still damp, musty and cold.

Every night, Christine would cuddle up to her parents, listening to the grim rumbling sound of the bombers and the explosions, shaking the ground more and more violently as they came closer and closer, before thankfully finally passing by. It was terrifying, and Christine would have difficulty holding back her screams as the bombs dropped around them.

In March 1941, there was a particularly dreadful raid on London, which included the use of firebombs. The next day, her parents sat her down and said,

"Last night was enough, Christy. You must move out of London. We have had a good life and want to look after our home and we will take our chances. You are still so young with a wonderful life ahead of you."

"You know your sister, Elsie, has trained as a nanny and is working for Lord and Lady Conway in Shropshire. Well, we have contacted the Conways, and they said they would be delighted to have you because they are running their huge house on less than the bare minimum of staff because of the war. On top of that, they are giving temporary homes to at least ten children who had been evacuated there from Birmingham."

Tears welled up in Christine's eyes. "I don't want to leave you; I won't!" Her Mum said, "You must, Christine."

Christine hugged her mum and cried and cried. After the sobs had died down, she said reluctantly,

"Ok, I'll go, and I understand, but I will worry about you every day, facing the continuing raids."

Little did she know at that moment in time that moving to join her sister would change her life in so many ways. She met Sam while working for the Conways, and although she was always worried about what was happening in the war, and her parents in London, it became a happy time for Christine. They were treated well. She was with her beloved sister, and she met Sam, and their romance blossomed.

When Sam enlisted and went off for his training in June 1942, Christine and Elsie decided they needed to do more for the war effort and enlisted in the Land Army. Christine had to wait for six months before she was old enough to join and return to London while she waited. Unfortunately, she was posted to a different part of the country from Elsie, who was now in Wales, while she ended up in Suffolk at the beginning of January 1943.

It would have been better in many ways had she not experienced the blitz first hand and known the terrors it brought, as it would make her worry even more about her parents while she was away. She longed for the world to calm down from its frightening chaos. She wanted things to be just ok again. She longed for peace, to be with her family, and maybe to settle down hopefully with Sam and have a family of her own, and just live the normal life she had dreamed of as a child. This seemed an unlikely prospect in the foreseeable future.

She was brought to earth from her thoughts as she suddenly noticed Mrs Piper entering the field, which was unexpected as she rarely came out into the fields. She thought little more about it, though, as she again became engrossed in her work. When she next lifted her head, she realised she seemed to be walking directly towards her. Christine smiled and acknowledged her with a nod. Mrs Piper, however, did not return the gesture or hold her gaze and looked down at the ground. It was then that a pang of cold fear shivered through her. The bombers, ready for their missions, quickly disappeared into the distance, leaving silence. She waited in a cold, silent, grey anticipation that echoed the mood of the sky.

Her ordinary routine day was about to become anything but, and for reasons she dreaded.

Chapter 3.   Shropshire June 1942

Children, and to a lesser extent families, were evacuated from industrial cities to the countryside. It was thought they would be safe from aerial bombing there.

Those living in the countryside saw an influx of women and children. Many of these children would stay with middle and upper-class families.

Many were surprised and shocked by the conditions of the people arriving from the industrial cities, especially the children. City children often had poor clothing and were sometimes dressed in rags. They suffered from developmental illnesses such as polio and rickets. They were often poorly educated and had suffered from a lack of clean air.

Evacuation helped to change attitudes because it meant that working-class children mixed with more affluent families. It highlighted the severe poverty that still existed in cities after the reforms of the early 1900s. Upper and lower-class citizens were brought closer together.

The train pulled into the station with a series of jolts, screeching brakes and bursts of steam and smoke. The steam engine was like a powerful living creature, letting out one huge last long breath as it came to a halt.

Christine started to get ready to disembark. She would have normally been worried that this was indeed Shrewsbury, as all the signs had been removed from the railway stations as a war precaution to confuse the Germans should they invade. Fortunately for her, an elderly doctor, who had sat opposite her since leaving Birmingham, was from the town, and it transpired, travelled there quite often to see his family. He had engaged her in a gentle and kindly conversation since joining the train, interested in her story.

"Don't look so worried", he said with a warm, sincere smile. "I'm sure I can help", Christine answered, a little tearfully. "I've left my parents in London to join my sister near a place called Shrewsbury at their insistence. They want me to be safe, but I'm so worried about them, and I'm going to be so far from home if something happens to them."

He said, "Look, my name's Doctor Denny, and who am I talking to." He said again in a reassuring way.

Christine smiled back through he tears and said, "My name's Christine and going to stay with my sister, Elsie, with the Conways at their house."

"Well, I'm sure it's for the best. You will love the countryside, and I'm sure you'll love seeing your sister. We have had some bombing raids in Birmingham but nothing on the scale of London yet. You are very brave to be making this journey. How old are you?"

"Fifteen", she replied, "but nearly sixteen."

He said, "look, don't worry. I'm going your way, and I'll make sure you get off at the right stop."

Christine felt a lot better now she had someone to help her, and they both chatted away about their lives until he said:

"Well, we will be coming into Shrewsbury soon. It's been lovely to talk to you, and I'm sure everything will turn out well."

He helped her with luggage. It consisted of a battered old brown leather suitcase. It contained the bare minimum of clothes. The doctor helped her lift it from the train, and she thanked him and wished him well, too.

She stood on the platform with her luggage, nervously looking around. To her immense relief, waiting on the platform was what appeared to be Conway's chauffeur holding a cardboard sign with her name on it. He was a tall and wiry man dressed in a smart blue uniform with a peaked hat. After making her farewells and thanks to the doctor, she made her way to the waiting man and waved at him.

She knew she would like him at once as he waved back. He had a friendly, warm smile, twinkling grey eyes, thick grey hair with long sideburns, a droopy moustache and a tanned, ruddy complexion, which suggested he didn't spend all his time driving. He was, she guessed, in his late fifties. He held out his hand to shake hers and introduced himself in a strong midlands accent

"I'm Mr Gray luv, 'though call me George, everyone else doos."

She was initially a little disappointed her sister, Elsie, was not there to meet her and said that to him.

George said, "She 'ad to look after them kids this mornin'. She was sad not to come to the station, but she were bouncing up and down with excitement about yur comin."

He thankfully relieved her of her travel bag and started walking towards the station exit, talking all the time, a habit of his, she gradually realised. He had a thick Midlands accent, and it wasn't always easy to make out what he was saying.

"There's the cathedral over there by the river. Go past it on the way. Best one int the 'ole country. It's about a thirty-minute drive to the estate. It's a lovely country, though. Bin 'ere all me life. Don't even seem like there's even a war a going on here most times."

Outside the station, she looked around for a car. There was only one, and she realised with surprised and excited pleasure that they were walking towards it. It was a beautiful blue and black gleaming old Rolls Royce limousine. The sweeping curves of its wheel arches, its large, shiny grill and huge headlights give the car a certain personality and majesty. Christine gazed at it in awe and also surprise. Surprise because petrol had been scarce since the beginning of the war and now virtually no civilians travelled by car, as most had been commandeered for the war effort. Somehow, it seemed, the Conways had found a way around this, she thought, slightly annoyed, but not enough to not look forward to the ride.

He opened the door to the passenger seat with a "Make yourself comfy me duck." And, she got in, and he closed the door behind her. She had never been called 'me duck' before, and it sounded more like the word 'book' but beginning with a 'd' not a 'b', but she realised it was a term of endearment, and she liked it. While he put the luggage in the back, she looked around. The seats were of polished leather, which squeaked as she moved and the smell of the leather combined with a whiff of tobacco. A pipe and tobacco pouch were, she noticed, stored in the central compartment.

George got in alongside her, and the car started effortlessly, and they moved off quietly and smoothly down the road and out of Shrewsbury. Riding in a Rolls Royce was an absolute luxury, and she loved it after the uncomfortable, long, busy train journey from London. The cathedral was indeed impressive, but coming from

London, it was nothing compared to St Paul or Westminster Abbey, she thought, though she didn't say that to George, of course.

They whisked smoothly and sedately along the country lanes with George chattering away. She enjoyed his chatter, although she didn't always understand what he was talking about through his strong accent. She was so excited, though, and was longing to see her sister. Elsie was clearly enjoying life working as a nanny for the Conways, and they had shared many letters. Whilst the Conway's two children were now grown up, they had taken in ten children, all under eight, and evacuees from Birmingham and more were expected soon. The family were very kind, she said and treated her almost like one of them. They lived in a large old manor house and owned many of the farms around.

After about half an hour of gliding through the country lanes, a large, imposing house came into view. It was a three-story red brick building, and she counted in wonder thirty-three windows on the front of the building. George pointed to it and smiled.

"That'll be your new 'ome."

As more of the manor came into view, Christine realised that not only was there a large manor house but also numerous outbuildings.

"Used to be a staff of twenty workin' for them," continued George as if reading her thoughts, "but now most of the bedrooms are closed down as there ain't enough help to manage them all."

The car crunched on the gravel as they turned into the long drive leading up to the house. As they proceeded up the drive, they passed a group of men of various ages in uniform being drilled by an older man in a smarter uniform who, she guessed, must be their commander.

"That's the Home Guard on parade, and his lordship is in charge," smiled George with a wink, "Just hope we don't have to rely on them."

One of the younger men, in particular, looked her way with interest, and she quickly turned away, slightly flushed, as the car moved on and came to a gravelly crunching halt outside the main door.

The door opened, and there was her sister, Elsie, smiling from ear to ear. She ran up to the car and opened the passenger door before George had had a chance to do so. Christine virtually jumped out, and they gave each other a huge hug. It was just so good to see her, and apart from looking a little more tanned, she was still her sweet loving, protective, wonderful sister. Elsie has bombarded her with all sorts of questions about her journey, their parents and the bombing

"Slow down, slow down," laughed Christine.

"Ok sorry, you must be so tired. But really, how's mum and dad? I bet the bombing must be scary."

"They're fine. You know our Mum and Dad; they would never let you know even if they weren't. The bombing has died down a little, and at least it's not every night now, which is a huge relief," replied Christine.

"Follow me, Sis. I'll let you tell me all about it later," said Elsie, "And I'll show you where we are staying. We are sharing a room together. It's a huge place, and most of the rooms are empty. The evacuees are great, and we've had four new arrivals two days ago."

They walked along a long corridor, and the walls were covered with impressive portraits, presumably of Conway's predecessors, gazing down on them. It was slightly dusty, though, she noticed, and the corridors had a musty smell about them. She guessed this might be because, as George had said, they no longer had enough staff to manage the upkeep because of the war.

They came out of the back of the main building into a smaller annexe.

"That's where we are, sis," smiled Elsie. "It will be so lovely to have you with me; I have missed you so much."

"So have I. Life's not the same without my big sister to talk to."

Elsie stopped by a door and opened it. It was quite a large room with two neat beds in it and a basin in the corner. "Your's is that bed, sis, and the toilets are just down the corridor. We have hot water in the evening and most mornings, too! I suggest you have a rest now. There's nothing that needs doing for now, and I'll wake you when its time for supper. We have it with the kids, so I can introduce them to you, then."

With another great sisterly hug, Christine gratefully sat on the bed, took her shoes off, and her hot feet enjoyed the cool freedom. Elsie left the room with a caring, smiling look, and Christine collapsed onto the bed a soon gratefully fell asleep.

She was woken an hour or so later by Elsie's nudge, and she smiled as she realised where she was.

"I had such a good sleep," said Christine. "Just what I needed."

'Well, it's nearly dinnertime, and we have some new kids to look after. They haven't even seen the country before, so you'll have to be very understanding."

"I'll follow your lead, Els'. Just show me what to do. Poor mites, it must be hard for them. I know what it was like for me."

Christine quickly washed and dressed and then followed Elsie down the corridor into a large dining room where a group of twelve kids aged between seven and twelve were sitting around two tables. Elsie had already organised it so that the newcomers were mixed with older kids who had already been at the Hall for sometime.

"This is Christine, my sister from London, and she's here to help me look after you. She's lived in London during the bombing, so she knows what it's like and what some of you have been through."

"I 'ate 'Itler," shouted out one of the boys. "He bombed our chip shop."

"He ain't so bad," said another. "They bombed our school, too, so we didn't have to go for a few weeks."

"Now quieten down," said Elsie, "And you who have been here longer make sure the new children know how things are done around here."

They all settled into eating their food and chatting quietly. Christine and Elsie sat at another table and kept a watch over them, making sure the new and younger ones were ok.

A typical day looking after the children turned out to be ensuring they got up and went to the local school, and then things like giving the children chores to do, for example, daily feeding the hens and ducks and collecting the eggs. It was always a problem and also lots of fun when the ducks escaped onto the lake, for it was a long-winded task to persuade them back in.

The Conways also kept pigs, and they were allowed to kill one per year. On the day the local butcher came to kill a pig, Christine and Elsie took the kids off with sandwiches and a drink to spend the day up in the countryside away from the noise and sights that might upset them. Some days, the children's parents made trips to see their offspring, so Elsie and Christine managed to hear something of the devastation of Birmingham by the bombing.

The garage where bikes were kept was George's domain. Christine had decided to go to the local small town of Shifnal, about six miles way, to run some errands, so she asked George to borrow a bike. George scratched his head thinking as if it was a difficult question.

"We ave one, but it be a bit on the old-fashioned side," said George. "I'm a mendin' the one your sister uses; it's got a flat tyre, must be a puncture." He said rather obviously. "Ere use this ole one; she's a bit on 'eavy side but still goes alright, in a straight line anyway," He said with a smile.

"Thanks, George, I'm sure she'll be fine," she said determinedly but now a little dubiously.

"Just take it easy mind."

"I'm good on a bike," Christine added, more to herself than George.

It was a certainly very heavy old bike, thought Christine as she lifted it upright. At least it had a wicker basket on the front. She had learned to ride a bike in London. Her Dad was an enthusiastic bike rider, and when they went on holiday by train, he would often ride his bike down and join them later. Although the roads were much busier in London, where she learnt, this heavy monster was designed for a man. It was different to the one she had learned on. Since she had asked George, and it was now a bit difficult to change her mind as he was watching, she reluctantly decided to follow through with her original plan.

She managed to get on and rather wobbly started off down the gravel drive. As she gathered speed, however, she quickly realised that the brakes were rather optimistically named so, and she increasingly gathered speed as she rolled down the drive. Her hope was to stay on until the drive flattened out. Half way down, however, the drive curved. As luck would have it, assembled there today were the home guard being drilled by Lord Conway. She started to panic as she realised negotiating the bend and missing the men was likely to be somewhat of a challenge. Closing in on the men on parade, she finally lost balance trying to achieve this feat, and the bike careered out of control and crashed into the bushes on the far side of the bend.

Some of the men rushed over to help. One of them, Sam, she later discovered, helped her up and recovered the bike for her. He had a friendly demeanour, and, as well as being embarrassed, she blushed even deeper in the presence of this good-looking young man. Sam appeared not to notice.

"Are you alright? That was quite a fall. The gravel is not very easy to ride on, especially on that old thing." He said kindly. "You look like you have grazed your knee. Here, borrow my hanky; it's clean."

"I'm uh fine, just a little bit shaken. Thank you so much."

"The bike's ok," he said, inspecting it. "Not built for that speed, though."

She tied the hanky quickly around her knee, and flustered, she remounted the bike, anxious to depart the scene of her embarrassment. She cycled off slightly unsteadily but could not resist a quick glance back, only to see Sam staring after her as he walked back the parade.

When she got back later that day after a thankfully uneventful trip, Elsie already knew all about her crash in front of the Home Guard. She said everyone had heard it from George.

"Don't worry, Sis, mind it could only happen to you. So, tell me about the nice-looking lad who helped you. Oh, and let's have a look at that graze of yours."

"He was nice, but I was too embarrassed to say anything sensible. I just wanted to get away without everyone seeing how much I blushed."

"Perhaps, he'll be at the dance in Newport on Saturday," said Elsie, re-bandaging Christine's knee "Mmm", replied Christine wistfully.

Elsie just smiled fondly as she finished her medical work.

The nearest the evacuees came to an actual experience of war whilst at the Conways was one afternoon when they saw in the distance a German aircraft falling out of the sky in flames. The pilot baled out, and his parachute opened. His plane had obviously been way off course, probably returning from a raid on Liverpool or maybe Manchester. Christine, having seen plane crashes happen quite often in London, also saw an opportunity and shouted to Elsie;

"Come on, Sis, those parachutes are made of real silk. We can use it for all sorts of things. Grab some pitchforks, and let's get George, too."

Soon Elsie, Christine, George, three other women from the house and the evacuees were running helter-skelter across the fields to see what had happened. The German airman was obviously uninjured, as he at once panicked when he saw them and ran off towards the woods. He soon glumly remerged, however, looking terrified, having been captured by local farm workers, who proudly had surrounded him with pitchforks and an array of farm implements. They were prodding him and baiting him with their implements. Christine couldn't bear it. She ran across to them and told them to leave him alone.

"He's probably a family man like you with kids at home. Would you want your sons and brothers in the army to be treated this way if they were captured?" She said, trembling and slightly taken aback by her own actions.

The men, slightly shocked by the outburst from this young woman, shamefacedly stopped and guarded him more passively.

"Well done, little Sis. I'm really proud of you," said Elsie, giving her a comforting hug. It wasn't long before Lord Conway arrived with a detachment of Home Guard, and Christine was pleased to see Sam was part of the group. Lord Conway congratulated them on their brave actions, although he said, rather self-importantly, that it was perhaps a foolhardy thing to do and perhaps they should have waited for the Home Guard. Sam and Christine exchanged glances and smiles before they marched the poor airman away.

Christine, Elsie and the children then gratefully gathered up the parachute and marched triumphantly back to the house. The kids were full of excitement and wanted to write letters straight away to their parents telling them of their heroic deeds.

"There will be enough material to provide silk bloomers for all the women in the village," exclaimed Christine happily.

Parachutes would provide precious silk for them to make underwear out of, a rare luxury during the war. All the families in the village who wanted some silk were given a share, but others would not touch it because it was German.

Elsie, who was an expert with a sewing machine, soon made some underwear out of her and Christine's cut. Christine also saved a piece that had some German printing on it. It was unusable, and she decided to keep it anyway as a memento of the day.

The following Saturday, they cycled to the dance. It was still blackout, and even their lamps were painted over apart from a thin slit. If there was no moon, they could hardly see their way, but luckily, that evening, it was bright and full, and the sky was cloudless. The smells of the countryside and the noises of night animals and birds had been slightly disturbing to a city girl like Christine at first, but she had gradually become used to them and now enjoyed listening out to identify what she could hear. They reached Newport uneventfully and left their bikes outside the dance hall.

It was a small hall, and the dance had obviously been organised by the local vicar, who was sitting in the corner keeping a watchful eye on proceedings. Christine and Elsie might well have been seen as interlopers at such an affair, but the combination of the huge changes caused by the war, the fact that Elsie had been there before and news of their parachute exploit and their generosity in sharing the spoils, ensured they received a warm welcome from the other local girls.

Refreshments consisted of a fruit punch, though it seemed from the behaviour of the local lads who regularly popped outside that sometimes something stronger might be added. The girls all sat at one side of the room, and the boys, as they entered sat on the opposite side. The music, it appeared, was to be provided by a local ensemble consisting of an aged, grey-haired man on the piano, a slightly younger violinist and a drummer.

Soon, the music began, and initially, the girls danced together to the slow waltzes that seemed to be the forte, and probably the only repertoire, of the musicians. The boys watched from their chairs until some of them summoned up the courage to ask the girls to dance. It wasn't long before Christine noticed Sam coming across the room to her as she was taking a rest from her first couple of dances. She felt a slight twinge of excitement combined with a slight flush of embarrassment. She blushed, annoyingly, very easily.

"Hello, Christine," he said. "How's the leg? One of the lads in the Home Guard told me your name."

"Oh, it was nothing really. The embarrassment hurt more than my knee." She smiled nervously.

"That's good. Then you are alright to dance?" "I'd love to," said Christine.

Soon, they were following the clockwise procession around the dance floor and Sam, she soon found out, was a very good dancer.

"Where did you learn to dance so well?" asked Christine.

"I have four big sisters, so they give me plenty of practice because they always needed a male partner."

"Four!" exclaimed Christine

"Yes, and three brothers, too. I am the second youngest. That's my youngest sister Evelyn over there. Do you have sisters and brothers?"

"Just my lovely sister, Elsie. We are so lucky to be together here and away from London, where my parents live."

"Must be very worrying for you from the reports of all the bombing" "Yes, terribly," said Christine.

"You are gaining quite a reputation, it appears" "In what way," said Christine, looking up at him.

"Well, bike crashes, capturing German airmen and providing silk to the village."

Christine smiled and again blushed slightly. They talked as they danced and then danced and talked some more. They both found conversation easy, and time passed quickly. When the evening came to an end, Sam asked her if perhaps she would like to go for a walk and a picnic when she was free. She happily agreed and the fixed it for the following Sunday week.

As soon as she got back to Elsie, she was grilled about what they had talked about. Elsie was always popular with the boys and had been dancing all evening, too, but with no one in particular. Christine told her everything they had talked about while Elsie sat there listening happily to her obviously happy sister.

"You don't think it's a bit to forward to go out for a walk with him next Sunday, do you?" said Christine.

"No, of course not. Everyone knows everyone around here. It will be fine."

As they cycled back to the Conways that night, Christine thought she had never enjoyed the countryside and its smells and noises as much. She was really looking forward to seeing Sam again.

The following week seemed to drag by and although she hoped she might catch sight of Sam on parade with the Home Guard, it was not to be. She was kept busy with the children as it was their half term, and she and Elsie were the main source of entertainment for them.

The following Sunday, Sam came to meet her at the Conway's on his bike. Elsie was with Christine when she arrived, and Christine introduced him.

"Just you look after my sister Sam, or you'll have me to deal with," she said slightly fiercely.

Sam, taken slightly aback, replied that of course he would, and then Elsie smiled and they all relaxed. They all chatted for a while before Christine and Sam cycled off down the drive. They chatted with each other about their respective weeks before Sam indicated they should turn through a gate and into a field.

"We can leave the bikes here and walk for a bit," said Sam. "It's about a mile's walk from here, but it's a lovely spot, and we can see the Wrekin, an unusual hill, from there."

As they walked, Christine was impressed with Sam's knowledge of the countryside animals, birds, flowers and plants. He seemed to know the song of most birds and would stop Christine and ask her to listen to one he recognised. Soon, they reached the spot Sam had chosen for their picnic.

"I've brought some sandwiches, a couple of apples and some sponge cake I made," said Christine.

Sam produced a blanket from is backpack and laid it on the ground while Christine set out the plates and food.

"Quite a spread!" said Sam. "Quite a view," replied Christine.

Sam explained that the Wrekin, the lonely hill they could see was the end of a chain of hills, called 'The Long Mynd.' He said that his Grandmother was Welsh, and the name meant 'Long Mountain' or 'long hill.'

"It's a local landmark around here," he said, "And when someone is taking a long time to explain something, locals will say he's going around the Wrekin."

"A little like you are now," teased Christine.

Sam laughed. He had an easy manner and rarely took offence it seemed. Christine liked that about him. There were too many other difficult things going on in the world at the moment to worry about small things.

They talked about their families and backgrounds, which were similar in terms of close family but very different in terms of the environment they were raised in. Christine was a city girl, and Sam, a country lad. Sam said he had never been to London, and Christine told him about the things he was missing. Again, they talked for hours, and Sam suddenly realised the time.

"Good heavens, it's almost four o'clock," he said. "Time to get you back before I get in trouble with that sister of yours," he smiled.

As they caught each other's gaze, they lingered there a little too long, moved towards each other and gently kissed. When they withdrew, they looked at each other and smiled before repeating the experience. Christine had never kissed a boy before except her cousins, and the kiss filled her body with warmth and electricity. Sam, who had a little more experience with girls, knew this kiss was very different to anything else. They walked back, hand in hand, to the bikes, and Sam invited her to meet his family and have dinner the following Saturday. Christine agreed at once, and they cycled back to the Conway's. As they were in view of the house, they, more modestly, gave each other a hug and a simple kiss on the cheek as they said their goodbyes.

Elsie was full of questions on her return, and Christine blushed slightly as she told her of her day and the kiss that they had shared.

"It was like a tingle of electricity," she said wistfully remembering the kiss. Elsie could see that her sister was becoming besotted already.

"Just take is slowly, Sis. He seems a nice boy, but really, this is only your first boyfriend." She warned her gently, although she was delighted for them.

While food was never short in the countryside compared to the cities on rations, luxuries were still not easy to come by. Sam was determined that when Christine came to his parent's house, they would serve something special. Although they lived on the Conways' estates, they were not allowed to poach on their land, well, in theory, at least. Whilst they weren't supposed to at least go on to the estate land to catch pheasant, it was a different matter if the birds strayed into your garden.

Sam had devised a method years ago to keep them supplied with the occasional pheasant in season. He would lure the birds regularly into their garden through a hole in the hedge by leaving out a bowlful of dry currants. They would get used to visiting the garden for these occasional treats. When he wanted to catch one, he would soak the currants that night in some of his Dad's sloe gin. The following morning, there would be at least a couple of very drunk pheasants lying on their backs, and this morning did not disappoint. There were two lovely birds already marinated senseless in the garden. Sam picked them up and took them to his mum. They would be eating well tonight and he hoped this might impress Christine.

When Christine arrived the following weekend, Sam's parents immediately liked her when they met her, and it was mutual with her. She particularly liked Sam's sisters, Evelyn and Mary, and enjoyed the evening tremendously. She had never had pheasant before and loved the story of how Sam managed to catch them.

After the meal, Sam and Christine went outside. It was a wonderful, moonless evening, and the combination of blackout regulations and remote countryside enabled the evening sky to put on a magical display of the stars in all their glory. As they left the house, Sam gazed up into the heavens and exclaimed,

"What a wonderful night for star-gazing. I have always loved looking up at them. Over time, from my dad and a book from the library, I have learned where most of the constellations are and their names. See that one like a saucepan," he pointed northwards high in the sky, "that's the Great Bear. It's also called the Plough, but I like the Great Bear better. If you follow a line upwards from the last two stars, you get to Polaris, the North Star. That's the one sailors navigate by because it always stays in the same place, due north."

"My favourite though is Orion 'The Hunter'. It's easy to find. Look, those three stars make his belt. Then you can see the stars at the bottom of his armour with the bright one on the bottom right - that's called 'Riegel'. At either end of his shoulders are two stars. The bright one by his left shoulder is my favourite. It's slightly red, and it's called Beetlejuice."

"You are pulling my leg," said Christine. They wouldn't call a star Beetlejuice!"

"Ok well, its actually Betelgeuse," he smiled, "but for me, it's definitely 'Beetlejuice.' It's sometimes known as Orion's armpit, too. It's supposed to be 500 times bigger than our sun. I love it because of its name and colour."

They both gazed silently at it for a minute.

"Tell you what. Whatever happens to us in the next few confusing and scary years, whenever we look up and see 'Beetlejuice,' we'll smile and think of each other."

"Ok, we have a deal," said Christine. "Even if I'm not sure you're kidding me about the name," she smiled happily.

53

They looked at each other and then yielded to the charm of the moment, hugging and then kissing each other.

Over the following weeks and months, they saw each other as often as they could, and their relationship blossomed in line with the warming of the season. Sam was waiting to have his call-up papers soon, as he turned eighteen in June 1942, and sure enough, they arrived. To his surprise, he was to join a famous Regiment, The Royal London Irish Rifles, and undergo his training near Belfast. He was due to report to barracks north of Birmingham in ten days.

They both knew this was going to be a huge test of their relationship and that they would be unlikely to see each other again until Sam had his embarkation leave. And even then, this was only a sort of interlude before he would be shipped off to some dangerous battle front. Christine thought it was so unfair for their relationship to be disrupted in this way. Sam reminded her that if it wasn't for the war, they would never have met in the first place.

"Why are you so bloody sensible?" she told him

"Why are so bloody wonderful?" he replied with a wink. And they fell into each other's arms once again.

During the following days before he left for Belfast, they spent as much time as they could together. They both loved walking, and although Christine was a city girl, she was growing to love the countryside even more. Sam loved to explain the names of trees and birds to her, though she was always a bit doubtful about some of the names he told her. She would always check up when she got back from her time with him. He was always full of jokes and stories. On one trip, he pointed up at a few birds of prey circling menacingly in a field nearby.

"They are Red Kites," said Sam. "The other birds of prey you sometimes see are Buzzards. It's easy to tell the difference, though." He paused.

"Well, go on, tell me; don't keep me in suspense," said Christine.

"Well, they are similar looking, but you can always tell if it's a kite because it will have a string tied to it."

Christine nodded but was a little confused. She noticed Sam grinning and suddenly got the joke. She punched him playfully and then laughed with him. They made the most of the ten days before he left. They both knew that their relationship would have to undergo many challenges before the war was over. But at last, their blissful ten days came to an end, and it was time for Sam to leave for Belfast. They enjoyed a final emotional farewell picnic, and Christine hated to see him leave and broke down in tears. Sam held her closely, finding it hard not to cry, too.

"Don't come to the send-off in the village. It's going to be hard enough to leave you, so let's do it now."

And they did.

After Sam left, things got back to normal. The routine of every-day tasks kept them busy but not enough for Christine to miss Sam badly, and she thought of him on the ferry crossing to Belfast as she knew he hated the sea.

Christine and Elsie started to feel they needed to think about a change, too.

Chapter 4. London & Belfast 1943

In general, most Infantry recruits received six weeks basic plus another six of Infantry specific. Huge areas of the UK were taken over for this purpose with the local population evacuated. Severely bomb-damaged areas of cities were often used for training in street fighting, etc.

There would be lots of drills, PT, weapon training, route marching, etc. Infantry specific got more sophisticated as the war progressed.

Living conditions were Spartan, huts, if they were lucky, but often under canvas. Mattresses were usually straw-filled. Washing and hygiene facilities were, by modern standards, pretty basic.

Life was very hard during the Blitz and frightening, too. London, in particular, was very bad as it was bombed nearly every night. People in London spent most nights sleeping in Air Raid Shelters. No one within any distance of a likely target, such as a big city, could sleep entirely easily in their beds.

After Sam left for training in June 1943 with the Royal London Irish Rifles Regiment in Northern Ireland, Christine and Elsie found that the evacuees were also returning to their homes in the Midlands, as the threat of bombing had decreased since the Battle Of Britain. The Conways were very keen to keep them on and help them look after the manor house. They even offered them a small cottage they could have rent free if they would stay. Both Christine and Elsie had already decided, though, that they wanted to contribute more towards the war effort, especially as it didn't feel right, as nice as the Conways had been, to work for rich country people when the world was at war.

Glamorous posters were also appearing, showing women working on farms as part of the Women's Land Army. Both of them thought this looked very exciting and would give them a chance to help feed Britain and make a difference. Women had to be eighteen to join and didn't need any experience, and while Elsie was now already eighteen years old, Christine had another six months to go.

They both applied, and Elsie was immediately accepted while Christine only provisionally so and would have to wait until she was eighteen. Elsie was sent for training and posted to work on farms near Cardiff in South Wales. This was quite a coincidence as Sam would sail to North Africa from Cardiff some months later, and Cardiff she would find was to play an important role in her life.

Christine decided to go back to London for a while to work as a nanny for some friends of her parents. The blitz was finally over, and London was a safe place to live, though hugely disfigured by the bombing. There were still very sporadic raids but nothing on the scale of the blitz during 1940. These sporadic raids involved fewer planes, though it seemed they used increasingly larger bombs, and after every attack, Christine read about another part of London that had been hit and the damage done. These sporadic raids, to some extent, caused more fear than the regular raids because of their unpredictability.

It was still wonderful to return home to London, though. The bombing, though still causing havoc, was now more sporadic and targeted less at residential areas. People seemed to find ways of getting on with their lives. In fact, it became a badge of pride to do so. Christine found a job acting as a Nanny to her parent's friend's child to fill the time before she was able to join the WLA. This was not full-time, and as a result, part-time, she managed to finish her nanny qualifications at the local college.

When Sam received his call-up papers, he first had to go to Birmingham for a medical examination. Although he had a slight problem with the hearing in his left ear due to his childhood near-drowning experience, he passed A1. He then received a train warrant and instructions to report to St Lucia Barracks, Omagh, in Northern Ireland, in seven days' time, on 8th July 1943, for eight weeks of basic training.

The train took him to Liverpool, and then he boarded the ferry to Belfast. He hated the sea, and the ferry journey, although not that rough, made him seasick, not helped by the smell of greasy fried spam and chips being served for lunch. He was delighted to enter the calmer waters of Belfast Lough and finally see the black Harland and Wolf cranes of the port of Belfast looming up in front.

When the ferry docked at Belfast Ferry port, he disembarked with the others. The port was full of ships loading and unloading. It was difficult, with noise and commotion, to work out where they were all supposed to go. But before he had much time to look around, there was a 'Rifles' corporal shouting for any recruits for the camp to go outside and board the waiting army lorries. They were full of young, anxious men just like him and many away from home for the first time, just like him. They nodded to each other, but there was little conversation.

As they approached the camp, which consisted of lines of metal huts, he was surprised to see soldiers with rifles and steel helmets running through a wet field nearby and throwing themselves down every few yards. Sam felt this did not seem a very healthy or particularly sensible thing to do, but he later discovered that throwing yourself down in the cold and wet was the best bit because then, at least, you grabbed a little rest.

He was allocated to a hut and told to put his belongings in one of the two-tier bunks. Sam looked around and found that all the upper bunks were taken and he had to make do with a lower bunk.

The sergeant suddenly busted in through the door,

> "Right, you 'orrible lot, this is no 'oliday camp. Fall in outside at the double, and let's get you sorted out."

Sam lined up outside with the others. There, they were given a knife, fork and spoon each and then marched to a long dining room full of very noisy solders all clad in denim, which he found out was the working uniform of the time. He queued up with the others and was handed out a meal consisting of re-constituted potato, boiled tasteless haricot beans and a piece of tough, stringy meat. As he looked at this unappetising mess, he thought about leaving it, but the men around were shouting for none of them to throw anything away but to scrape it onto their plates instead. He assumed this was as good as it got and ate it without much enthusiasm. Outside the hut was a large tank full of boiling water where he had to plunge his eating irons in to wash them.

> "Right, you lot, back to your bunks. You're going to need all the sleep you can get," the sergeant barked.

They were then marched back to their hut for the first night on a hard camp bed with a pillow filled with straw and three army blankets. Sam lay on his bunk. He felt a mixture of anxiousness combined with excitement. His life so far had been cosy and supported, but breaking out of that routine made him realise how little of the world he had seen and that he found excited him.

Reveille, as he found out was the name for getting up and awake time, was at six the following morning, followed by a difficult shave in a room full of jesting squaddies, some of whom used cutthroat razors. Later, they were taken down to the stores where they were issued with two battle dress uniforms, an overcoat, a respirator, denims, two pairs of boots and all accoutrements required for soldiering. Then to the barbers where his head was shaved to a stubble with all the rest. Sam was then issued with an identity disc with his number on it, together with a rifle. The sergeant told them that the rifle, a Royal Enfield, was their most important item of kit.

"It may mean being killed or saved. It's you, your first line of defence against the enemy."

Every day during the six-week basic training, Sam felt they were just rushed from pillar to post, never having a minute until lights out at ten in the evening. Each day consisted of a mixture of continual rifle drills, physical training, Bren gun training and marching, which was always at a very fast pace.

Each Saturday morning, they were inoculated against various diseases. Sam would line up in a queue with his sleeve rolled up to reveal his bared arm. One by one, a fierce-looking nurse plunged a large, seemingly blunt needle into his arm. Some men actually fainted during this procedure, but luckily, Sam was not one of them. His arm was very sore and tender for most of the weekend. Soon, Monday came along again, and it was more marching, rifle drill, etc.

Sam also had to attend the hated dentist for treatment. After much uncomfortable poking around, the dentist decided that he needed a tooth out. After a painful struggle, it came out. All day long, it kept bleeding, and when he lay on his bunk that night, it still bled, so he had to get up to report to the Medical Orderly room. He knocked up the corporal on duty, and after inspecting the bloody hole in his gum, he rang for a medical officer who came and plugged the hole with cotton wool and instructed him to stay the night in the medical centre. This seemed heavenly, as it was a lovely soft bed with clean white sheets and white pillows.

One day, they were issued with two Mills Fragmentation bombs. These looked like metal pineapples with a locked metal handle on the side. Arriving breathless and sweating from a forced march to the practice ground in full kit with rifles, respirators, steel helmets, etc., they then had to wait their turn to go into the sandbagged throwing bays. In these throwing bays, there were two NCOs giving instructions, and they then took two men at a time to practice throwing the grenades. For some uncanny reason, when Sam's time came, he invited the man next to him to go first so that he could have a longer break to recover from the march. His replacement, while preparing to throw the grenade, dropped it in the mud in the throwing bay. It exploded, resulting in both soldiers and the NCOs being taken to hospital with nasty shrapnel wounds. While he was uninjured, it still shook him up. Perhaps he was to be a lucky soldier, he thought.

During his time in training, he became very friendly with his upper bunkmate, Fergus, who was a native of County Omagh. They shared a similar sense of humour and fun, and Fergus was a country boy just like Sam.

One evening, while lying in their bunks, they were sharing their knowledge and interest in the countryside.

"Ok then, Fergus, how do you tell the difference between a Buzzard and a Red Kite?" Fergus thought for a while. "Is it something to do with the shape of their tails?"

"Na," said Sam. "You can always tell a Kite cos it's got a bit of string tied to it."

Fergus looked puzzled for a moment, then burst into laughter

"I'll get you back for that, mucker," he said through his tears of laughter and threw one of his boots at him.

After three weeks, they had a weekend leave, and as this was too short a time to get home or see Christine, Fergus invited him to his home for the weekend.

They lived in a small neat farm near Loch Neagh and farmed dairy cattle. It was beautiful countryside, and Sam had never seen a lake that huge.

Fergus said, "Lough Neagh is the largest freshwater lake in the UK and Ireland. According to Irish legends, it was created when the giant Finn McCool scooped up a clod of soil. He threw the clod into the Irish Sea and became the Isle of Man."

"Yes, of course, Fergus," Sam smiled.

Fergus' parents were very friendly and made Sam feel very welcome. Being a dairy farm, they had access to a few more luxuries than those on rationing and he and Fergus were especially indulged while they were there.

For breakfast, Sam was served Champ. They all watched him to see his reaction. "What is it?"

"It's made with potatoes, milk, butter and scallions. We mash the potatoes with milk and chopped onions, and we cook to serve the best champ there is," said Fergus' Mum proudly.

Sam tentatively ate a spoonful and loved it.

All too soon, the break ended, and they had to return to camp. Sam thanked Fergus' family, and they left well-refreshed. Sam realised how little he had seen of the world and vowed to himself to see more if he survived.

On arrival back at the camp, they were given extra duties. This, they were told was because a party of War Office bigwigs was expected. They were told that officers of 'field rank' had to be greeted with 'present arms' by sentries. As a result, they were told to maintain a 24-hour guard at the various entrances to the camp for one week. Their sergeant, a veteran from the First World War by the name of Jones, or 'Jonesy' as they named him, told them to practice arms drill when night fell, as their ineptitude would go unnoticed. One night, a lad by the name of Gordon Lewis returned to the guardroom in a state of panic. Leaving his post without permission was crime enough, but this unfortunate lad had compounded the offence.

"I was practising 'slope arms'," he stuttered to the sergeant, "When I threw the thing over my shoulder and into the thick bushes. I can't find it, especially in the dark."

The sergeant then marched the 'criminal' back to the scene of the crime and began a search. Torches were forbidden in the blackout, and they could not find that rifle. When the orderly officer would make his rounds every morning, each rifle would be examined, and the loss would be exposed, causing trouble for all, including the Sergeant.

"I have an idea, Sarge," said Sam, and he explained it to Sergeant Jones. Jones had already noticed Sam and how he was respected by the other men, and as he was a great improviser, he straightaway organised for the plan to be put into action. The idea was that after the officer had inspected the first guard post, the soldier would have to run at great speed around the compound to the next gate and deliver his own rifle to Lewis before the officer arrived. The ruse succeeded, and face was saved. Lewis could not be charged either, as this would involve Jonesy's subterfuge being uncovered. The missing rifle was found later that morning, and Sam received a pat on the back from Jonesy and the others

"Thanks, Sam, you saved my bacon," Gordon said as he patted Sam on the shoulder. Christine and Sam wrote to each other often, and she learned all about his training and his life and exploits in Northern Ireland. She shared them with her parents, who particularly enjoyed and laughed at the missing rifle story. Her dad was full of stories, too, from his service in WW1, where he had been invalided out after a year with a knee injury that left him with a slight limp. He was always willing to show his kids the round, deep bullet hole scar on his knee and dare them to put their finger into it.

The dreadful bombing raids continued intermittently, and after one particular week of raids, she began to long for an undisturbed night and a good night's sleep. She still had to get up and travel to work after a terrible night and wend her way to the Jennings house, experiencing countless difficulties. Quite often, she could not to go by train as stations had been bombed, nor by bus as there might be unexploded bombs in the road.

Christine, like a lot of people, used to get lifts from whoever could take her. Lorry drivers would be very kind, and many times, she got in the back of one of their vehicles with lots of others in the same predicament. One day, she had to hang onto straps, where they usually hung the bacon, in the back of a Danish Bacon lorry.

Occasionally, she would arrive home after a day's work after a difficult journey and have to go straight into the shelter with her dinner handed to her by her Mum.

In the East End of London, it was a lot worse for families, as they were being targeted mercilessly by the bombing raids. It would break her heart to see them queuing on a lovely, hot summer's afternoon to secure a place in the Underground. When Christine was going to work, she would get off the underground railway and sometimes practically have to step over the people lying on the platform. Later on, she was thankful that conditions down there improved, bunks were built and facilities for food and drinks were on hand.

It was amazing, though given all the disruption, how some things seemed to go on as normal. A number of cinemas and theatres were still open, and people prided themselves on getting to work on time, whatever time they had to start in the morning.

One evening she arranged to go to a cinema with her friend Jennifer to see 'Casablanca' starring Humphrey Bogart and Ingrid Bergman. They thoroughly enjoyed the film, but on the walk home, as they were discussing it, they were stopped by a policeman and made to go down into the Public Shelter and could not leave until the 'All Clear' sounded. It was most uncomfortable and cold, and when she arrived home, she was then told off by her worried but relieved parents for being out all night.

Sam returned from his training and came to visit her in London on his embarkation leave. They only had a short time together, and it was worrying for both of them because he was not told where he was going. They had about a week together, and she was able to show him around London.

Her parents loved Sam straight away. He was easygoing and had a real interest in other people. He was particularly interested in her Dad's war experiences, and she was aware that he probably kept the worst of it from him so as not to worry Sam too much before he went. He won over her Mum very easily by enjoying her cooking and offering to wash up. Sam, being part of a large family, saw this as something he would often do at home, but her Mum was very traditional and declined the offer, although Christine could see how much this gesture pleased her

It was a dry, warm late summer that year, and in particular, they spent time walking in Regents Park and taking picnics with them. Christine did suggest going rowing on the Serpentine, but after Sam told her of his experience when he was young, she gave up trying to persuade him and gently teased him about it from time to time.

The week passed all too quickly, and they felt their feelings for each other growing stronger and stronger during those few days. They both loved each other's warmth and the fact that they were both very tactile and loved to hug and hold hands. Sam said that he was from a family of huggers, and he was delighted when he found out that hers was the same. She also discovered he was a great kisser, and when she commented on this, he said,

"Yes, while I've had so much experience. Must have kissed over two girls before you. And one of those was my sister for practice."

They both laughed and kissed long and sweetly in response.

On their walks through the park, they talked about their future and how difficult it might be to keep in contact.

"We must write as often as we can even if our letters don't always get through. I know I may be away for a year or maybe more, and I know you might meet many men while I'm away. If you do fall for one, don't tell me till I get home. I'm going to need my thoughts of you to help survive the difficult days ahead," Sam said.

"I think it's very unlikely that I'll meet anyone else, Sam. Like you, I'll be too preoccupied with surviving and helping out in the WLA. At least I have less to worry about, I think, as you'll be mostly surrounded by men." She smiled and kissed him gently on his forehead. "And if our letters don't get through, I'll just look up at Beetlejuice and think of you."

When it was time to part, it was a very sad moment. She went with him to Paddington station and waved him off in an emotional farewell. There were many other sad farewells at the station. She gave him a photograph of her in a beautiful envelope. He loved it and said that he would always keep it close to his heart.

The train engine gave a long, irritable hiss, seemingly anxious to be on its way. The guard blew his whistle and shouted all aboard. With a final long kiss and hug, Sam turned, threw his kit back over his shoulder and made his way into the carriage. The door closed, and Sam looked down at her from the open-door window they held hands for the last time until the train gathered speed, and they waved and waved till out of sight. They both wondered whether they would ever see each other again.

Christine slowly turned and left for home with tears in her eyes. She had held them back while with Sam, as she knew she had to be strong for him. The spring in her step during the last week had gone, and she almost felt her feet were too heavy to lift. She was determined to be strong, though, and if he could endure, then she certainly would and could.

Sam managed to find a seat on the crowded train his thoughts in turmoil. Why did it have to be that when he met someone he knew he could settle down with, this bloody war got in the way. On the other hand, he realised that without it, the chances that they would have met would have been very slim anyway.

After a two-and-a-half-hour journey, he arrived at Cardiff General Station. He had very little time to look around for as soon as he stepped onto the platform, he recognised a sergeant from his regiment shouting out for them all to assemble outside. They were then bundled onto trucks and taken down to Cardiff Docks.

The short journey to the docks went through an area known as Tiger Bay. He was astonished by the number of black people there. Whilst it was not the first time he had seen a black person, it was the first time he had seen them in such numbers. The area was poor, with lines of terraced houses.

The docks were a grim place. The area was dusty with coal dust and the smell from the nearby smoky steel works was pungent. When he looked out beyond the docks lock gates, all he could see were long stretches of mud, and he wondered how on earth the ship would get out.

They boarded a converted liner named the HMS Devonia. She had been painted grey as camouflage, enough hoped Sam to help them avoid danger. There were five other troop ships there, plus a number of Destroyers, presumably as escorts, he thought. They were shown to their accommodation where they were squashed in four to a small cabin.

"Where are the toilets?" said Sam after looking around.

"On deck!" said Fergus. It must be that a row of buckets with a plank resting on 'em with holes cut in it. Tell you what, I'll always make sure I'm in the middle of rough seas. The end guys may experience a shit wave."

Sam smiled grimly and already felt a little seasick before they left the docks. When they went up on deck later, amazingly, all that mud was now covered by the high tide. The bay was hardly recognisable. They sailed from Cardiff that evening in a huge convoy to hopefully counter some of the threat of U-boats. He had been especially nervous about this sea trip as he couldn't swim and had a fear of drowning. It wasn't long before he was seasick, and he suffered intermittently for the rest of the journey. Eventually, and thankfully, they arrived a few days later in the warm Mediterranean off the coast of Africa, they had been informed.

He wrote a letter to Christine telling her about his journey and arrival in North Africa, although it looked like he was in for another sea voyage to Italy soon. She received it a month later. Despite writing every week she found out later, he only received three during the whole war. It was a similar situation for her. She received two more before a long, uncertain and very worrying gap.

Chapter 5.   Stalag VIIIC

There were different types of POW camps in Germany, Poland, Czechoslovakia and Austria. Some were for non-officers called Stalags, some for officers called Oflags, some for airmen, Lufts and navy or merchantmen called Marlag Milags. They were usually divided into sectors by nationality. The Russians who had not signed the Geneva Convention were treated as 'political' prisoners, which gave the Nazis the excuse to treat them abominably.

Stalag VIIIC was a huge camp near Germany's border with Poland, housing 50,000 prisoners. It was close to Stalag Luft III, famous for 'The Great Escape.' Because of the physical restrictions of camp life and the crowded conditions, camps often fostered the ideal conditions for outbreaks of typhus, dysentery and diphtheria.

Red Cross parcels were key in supplementing diet and also making prisoners feel they were in contact with home. Approximately 163,000 parcels were made up each week.

The camp 'hospital' at Stalag VIIIC near Sagan in German Silesia near the then-Polish border was typical of most camps. It was located at a prudently isolated distance from the main gate. Cases of serious illness or injury used the main hut, but in another hut nearer to the gate was the Revier or sick bay, intended for recuperation or those with less serious complaints. Both were run by about forty trained, to some degree anyway, medical allied prisoners, a scattering of German medical staff and some of the recovering prisoners. They were a little different from the huts in the main camp, although they were kept warmer in the winter and generally had access to better rations. They were dull and grey outside and inside but at least smelt of clean, pungent disinfectant.

Inside the Revier, there were rows of bunks on either side. Some men were lying there asleep, and some were gathered together playing cards. It was late March, and the relentless winter was starting to make way for the promise of spring. The latest influx of prisoners here were from the battlefields of Italy, and they had undertaken a gruelling journey across the Alps in cattle trucks.

Sam awoke and was only hazily aware of his surroundings. He was very weak and had only just managed to survive a bout of dysentery he had contracted from the stinking marshes around Anzio. He was only just over eight and a half stone when he arrived and barely able to walk. Gradually, he became more conscious. One of his fellow prisoners noticed and came over with a cup of water.

"Drink up," he said, "it's important you get fluids inside you, the doctor said."

Sam drank up gratefully. His mouth felt like he had eaten gravel and tasted as if he had, too.

"Drink it slowly, lad. Let your body get used to it, or you'll be sick again."

He sat up, and Jimmy, the fellow prisoner's name it turned out, put some cushions behind him to support him.

"Just take it easy," he said.

"No need to talk. You've had a very rough time, but you're going to be ok."

And with that, he left him in peace. Sam sat there, taking it all in and trying to piece together what had happened to him since his capture at Anzio. Gradually, his memories came flooding back.

When the Germans first captured him and the other survivors, they searched them for arms and ammunition but made no attempt to take anything else from him, such as watches and pens. In this respect, they were far more disciplined than the average 'Tommy' that Sam had seen deal with German and Italian prisoners. They were then put into one of the rooms of the farmhouse with guards while they went to get instructions. Two or three of the guards proved very friendly. They tried to talk to him, but he knew no German and they little English. All they could manage were such expressions as,

"War no gut" and "For you, war is finish." If only that were true, thought Sam.

After this, they were given the job of carrying boxes of ammunition up to their front line. Whether this was permissible under the terms of the Geneva Convention, Sam didn't know, but he was in no position to argue the niceties of that Convention and did as he was told.

At that point, several Allied shells screamed over and exploded nearby. Sam remembered thinking that the Germans seemed to be more scared than he was. A whole line of German soldiers was spaced out, lying on the ground in the open and firing their rifles at random.

Sam and the other prisoners were told to pick up a stretcher bearing a wounded officer and carry him away from the line. As Sam and three others began to lift the stretcher, a stray bullet from the battlefield fizzed by, hit and wounded one of the Germans escorting them. He fell to the ground, screaming in pain and shock. The German soldiers, hyped up in the heat of the battle, were so enraged and scared at the same time that they wanted to respond immediately to something, anything. They saw Sam and his fellow prisoners and pointed their rifles at them as if about to fire. Sam crouched in fear and thought this was the end. Suddenly, their officer arrived. He quickly assessed the situation and barked loudly to the men to get back to their positions, shouting and pointing in the other direction,

"Der verdammte Feind sind die Idioten da draußen."

Although Sam couldn't understand exactly what he said, he got the gist, especially the idiot bit. After some hesitation, they did, too, and fortunately, came to their senses. As Sam realised he was safe, he regained his composure and realised that the German soldiers' actions were, of course, nothing to do with him directly. Maybe he thought he might have done the same in similar circumstances. The officer arranged for one of his men to give the wounded man was given a piggyback out of the line.

The officer indicated they should pick up the stretcher and follow him. As they walked along the German officer, quite a young man, started a conversation with Sam. He did not know any English, and he spoke no German, but they had both learnt a little French at school, and so they talked to each other in schoolboy French. They only mentioned their homes and families and, of course, did not touch on military matters. It was the first time he had had any kind of conversation with his enemy, and for the first time, it dawned on him that he could now see them as real individuals just like him.

Later, two, presumably intelligence staff, joined them. They questioned Sam in pigeon English about Allied artillery, and he was quite pleased he could honestly say he had no idea because they had been separated from the main division for almost a day. He was relieved when they left.

Eventually, they made their way to what seemed to be the German regimental H.Q., where they left the stretcher and its burden. Another officer gave instructions for one of the soldiers to escort them further. The soldier who had been detailed to do this began to walk down the road with his rifle slung over his shoulder. He had to keep looking back to make sure that his prisoners were following him. The officer noticed this and bellowed at the poor man to stop. He proceeded to give him an absolute dressing down. He should, of course, have walked behind them with his rifle at the ready so that he could easily see what was going on. It was strange, Sam recalled that even in the middle of all their uncertainty, they could laugh inwardly at this. He suddenly thought how Fergus would have laughed at that and felt very, very miserable.

So, they continued their walk along a long country road away from the front. At one point, they passed a motorcycle lying by the roadside with a dead dispatch rider by it, presumably a victim of Allied shelling and a grim reminder that they were not yet out of danger. Eventually, they came to a large, deep cave in the bare brown hillside. They were ordered inside and found it was already crowded with other British POWs, presumably captured earlier. At least it was shelter, and although they were physically and mentally exhausted after the events of the previous, they chatted with each other about their experiences and what might happen to them now.

Eventually, everyone settled into an uncomfortable and fitful sleep. What a day, he reflected shakily. So many horrific things had happened and shaken him to the core. As he was thinking through the events of the day, from the loss of his friend, to the encounter and death of the German soldier, the narrow escape from the grenade and the treatment he had at the hands of the Germans, he realised he was also seeing the enemy as real people and not simply an amorphous bunch of bloodthirsty men ready to kill him and anyone who got in the way of their conquering ambitions.

They spent an uncomfortable night in the cave, but Sam slept well from sheer physical and mental exhaustion. During the night, while he was asleep, someone stole a bar of chocolate from his haversack, which had been sent to him by his mother. He could have done with that, he remembered. He could almost taste the chocolate as he thought about it, and at least he realised that it was a sign he was feeling better and recovering some of his appetite now. It's strange the things he could recall. He did remember feeling that he now had a good chance of surviving the war. Before this and with the death of his close friend, he had practically begun to give up that hope.

A German sergeant entered shouting "Prost," and directed them to an area outside where there was a large tank of what he found to be very cold and not entirely clean water. Sam splashed his face gingerly. They were then fed some bread and, amazingly, some fresh tomatoes before being loaded onto awaiting lorries

They bumped along a rough road in what was now a hot sun. They then turned in through a guarded gate into what appeared to be a temporary prisoners camp. The POW 'camp' was large and in what seemed to be a film studio on the outskirts of Rome, and conditions were very crowded. No form of bedding was provided, so they stripped off sheets of the fibreglass noise insulation materials from the wall to lie on. Sam later realised the folly of what had seemed a good idea at the time, as fibres from the material would penetrate his clothes and were highly irritating for many days afterwards.

Loaded onto open trucks the next day, they were then driven around the streets of Rome. This seemed to be a propaganda exercise to impress the local Roman population with the number of prisoners that had been taken. Little in the way of enthusiastic cheering came from the crowds however, just curiosity. They did have a wonderful view of the magnificent ancient Roman Coliseum as the road circled around it. Sam hoped one day he would have the chance to tell Christine and his family about this experience.

The thought made him think about Christine. Was he idealising their relationship? They were both so young, and if she was experiencing even some of the terrors of war, how much would it change her? All he could do was hope for the best. It was no good fearing the worst. He had enough to cope with without adding any further misery.

They arrived at their next 'camp' near a railway siding yard. There were tents erected there for them to sleep, and the Germans provided them once again with some quite decent rations. This was the last food Sam remembered eating. Life after this became more and more hazy as he became increasingly ill. A few things later stuck in his memory although he would rather they didn't.

When he awoke the following day in the railway yard it was to the sound of a train squealing and screeching as it pulled in nearby. When one of the men looked out, he reported that it was pulling a long line of what appeared to be cattle trucks. Breakfast arrived, consisting of dry bread and olive oil, was circulated by the Germans but by this time, Sam could not manage a thing. He had already been sick, and his insides were starting to feel very uncomfortable.

The guards soon arrived and roughly bundled and squeezed them into the trucks. There was so little room and hardly any space for anyone to sit down not alone lie down. They devised a way of at least some of them sitting down in turns and using one corner of the truck as some kind of toilet, though the smell soon became almost intolerable. For the first time, Sam realised what captivity was all about. He had no control over anything. What he did, what he ate and when he did it was decided by someone else, and that 'someone' had little regard for his feelings or well-being. Of all the things he was to endure, this feeling of powerlessness was the most depressing and debilitating.

The train trundled and jerked along the tracks. Every jolt was proving a misery for Sam. On the second day of the journey, they heard the sound of a fighter plane overhead. The noise grew louder, and suddenly, they were under fire. It was obvious that what must have been an allied plane thought they were an enemy convoy of some kind. Bullets ripped through the carriages, and screams cried out as some of the men were hit. Thankfully, the sound of the plane's engine faded away, and at least it seemed it wasn't coming back for a second run at them.

Two men were injured, and the others did their best to help them. A few miles later, the train stopped, and the German guards took the injured off to what fate no one knew or liked to guess or had any energy to stop or protest about anyway. By now, personal survival was to the fore. Sam could remember very little of the four-day journey to what was to be his permanent camp, Stalag VIIIC, after that, except deliriously feeling so ill he just wanted to die

Finally, they arrived at the Stalag. Sam, by now, in a dreadfully weak state, was virtually carried off the train to a brick building where they were to be processed. They were told to strip completely, leaving their boots stashed in the room but tying their garments all in one bundle to be sent through a steam delouser. His fellow prisoners helped Sam, as he was now too weak to even manage this. They were then subjected to a fierce, very hot shower. They then had to wait shivering stark naked for a half hour in the waiting room until they were able to pick up their bundles of steaming clothes that had been processed.

Sam, supported to his feet by other men, was then fingerprinted, photographed, and issued metal 'Kriegsgefangene' dog tags with his new six-figure identification number. His name and identification number would be entered into a large ledger, from which a report of his imprisonment, he later found out, would be made eventually Allied authorities. Before his name entered that ledger, his family would have been told he was presumed dead or missing in action. Sam, now at the end of his tether and about to collapse, was put on a stretcher and taken to the hospital.

As he hazily reflected on what had happened to him, all he hoped for now was that he would survive the war and get back home. The simple joys of living in the countryside and the smell of hay at haymaking time, the fields after a rainstorm in the summer and his mother's homemade bread that he had taken for granted, he now longed for. He wondered where Christine was. Had she joined the Land Army? She had said she wanted to do more for the war effort. He admired those values in her and felt himself smiling as he thought of her. Given all the terrible events he had witnessed so far, he was not sure it was right to return to the simple country life he thought he longed for. He was beginning to realise that he wanted to make a difference and play his part in ensuring that wars like this never happened again.

The German camp doctor was doing his rounds and arrived at Sam's bed. He was a kindly-looking man in his late fifties. He was balding with a central flash of black hair swept back. He sat at Sam's bed.

"Hows are you, mein Sohn?" he said in his broken English. "I am feeling very weak," replied Sam.

"You must drink much Wasser und eat much but langsam, I means slow. If the guard asks you how you ist, you must say not gut. We must keep you here as long a time as we can so you get besser. I have a sohn who looks like you, and he is prisoner in England. I hope he is looked after too."

Sam smiled in response, and the kindly doctor moved on. The next few weeks vanished in a hazy state. He was visited, it seemed, by the doctor, and as he recovered his strength and his mind cleared, he started to chat with this friendly Doctor. They shared some of their backgrounds, and he could see how worried he was about his son and his family. The doctor told him quietly how he hated the Nazis and how most people hated him and his thugs too. He told Sam he had weighed only just over six stone when he arrived and needed time to build his strength

From time to time, a German officer would visit, point towards Sam and argue loudly, it seemed, with the Doctor. Sam managed to stay in the hospital for a whole month and gradually rebuilt his strength. He realised later that this period of recuperation probably saved his life, as without it, he would definitely not have withstood the challenges ahead. He also realised that without the doctor's protection, he would have been evicted from the hospital a lot earlier.

Eventually, the doctor could delay his eviction no longer, and along with several others, he was marched out of the hospital and into the camp. As they marched through the gate, Sam was amazed at how big it was and how many were imprisoned there. They were herded into an area in front of what seemed to be the German prison guards' HQ. They were told to stop and be silent. After a few minutes, an obviously more senior officer emerged and addressed them. The German commandant seemed to be rather a jolly fellow and could speak passable English.

"I am the camp commandant, and I bid you all a good morning," he said. All was silent in response.

"I say again, Good Morning."

At which a few mumbles issued from the prisoners in response. He seemed satisfied enough with this for now.

"You are here until the vor ist von. As long as you follow die Regen, then all will be gut. Remember, if any of you try to escape, you all get shot, understand, brrrrrr," he smiled, mimicking firing a machine gun. "Now you will go to ihre huts."

As they were led through the camp to their huts, Sam was amazed again at the size of the camp. It housed fifty thousand prisoners he later found out. Sam was allocated to hut seventeen and was escorted there by the hut leader, Sergeant Brian Elder.

"Call me Belter if you like he said – everyone else does. I will introduce you to your two 'muckers.' You work together to share chores and look out for and keep a watch on each other. Everyone is organised into small teams like this. Camp life takes a lot of getting used to, and if you have any questions or concerns then talk to me."

He could see the concern on Sam's face.

"We've all been through this adjusting process, and we all know what it's like. Hopefully, this bloody war won't last much longer, and we can get back to dear old Blighty. We just have to make the best of it, and in the meantime, we try and make the Goons' life as difficult as possible without getting them trigger-happy. Watch out for some of them as they are bloody sadists, but many of them are just like us, just wanting the war to be over."

They arrived at the hut, and Belter introduced him to his two muckers, Mick from Londonderry and Stan from South Wales. Stan was just a few years older than him with a shock of ginger hair and a face covered in freckles. He had a lopsided smile. Sam was relieved to realise that they would get on straight away. Mick was in his forties and had an air of quiet confidence. They took him to his bunk, and he was delighted to see he had a top bunk.

"We nabbed it for you. We knew you needed some TLC," smiled Stan.

Sam slung his kitbag onto the bunk and slowly climbed up; he was still weak. "Brew in about an hour when you can meet the others. Meanwhile, make yourself comfortable and relax. You'll do a lot of that around here as there's not that much else to do."

Sam did that. Opening his kitbag, he took out his photo of Christine from his tin box and wedged it between the wall and the end of his bunk beside him. It had now been fifteen months since he had seen her. Did she still think about him the way he thought about her? Did she and his family even know that he was still alive and not lying rotting in some gruesome battlefield? The thought of being forgotten was a depressing one. Not all pain is physical, he realised. He would prefer physical pain to the kind of inner trauma that haunted him at that moment. The feeling of hopelessness and alienation was a terrible prospect. He had been through the physical hurt, and he knew it would be easier to get over than the 'hidden' emotional hurt of feeling forgotten and having little control over his life. He would get through this somehow, and he had to believe that Christine would be waiting for him and feeling the same way, too.

Over the next few days, he gradually worked out how the camp was organised. The camp was divided into sectors that were allowed to mix during the day, except for those in the Russian sector. The Germans had separated off some huts to form their admin centre or Vorlager, where the Commandant had addressed them. The remaining huts were surrounded by a double row of barbed wire, about 4 metres high, with a gap of a metre between the rows. At ground level, between the rows, there were vicious coils of barbed wire. Within the perimeter, there was a wooden rail about half a metre from the ground and 3 metres from the wire. This was there to mark the limits of movement for prisoners, he was told

Over the next few months, he settled down into this POW non-life. They were fed almost the same food almost every day. Black bread, tea, tinned soup, potatoes and swede. Fortunately, the diet was supplemented with food items from the Red Cross parcels.

They received their Red Cross Food Parcels most weeks. The parcel was about a foot square and 6 inches high. It was meant in theory to last a week, but due to the lack of other food, in practice Sam might sometimes eat it all in two or three days and starve the other five or six. The Germans believed they could somehow use the canned goods for escaping purposes, so they punctured all canned goods and had to eat them quickly anyway. Generally, they would try and divide one parcel between six prisoners so that at the end of the sixth day, each man would have received a whole parcel.

Parcels could be from Britain, America or Canada and were all slightly different. They were distributed irrespective of nationality. A typical British parcel would contain ¼ ld. of tea, a tin of cocoa powder, a bar of chocolate (often Cadbury's fruit and nut), a tinned pudding, a tin of meat roll, a tin of processed cheese, a tin of condensed milk, a tin of dried eggs, A tin of sardines or herrings, a tin of preserve, a tin of margarine, a tin of sugar, a tin of vegetables, a tin of biscuits, a bar of soap and a tin of 50 cigarettes. Funnily, only the Scottish parcels contained rolled oats.

If it weren't for the food packages from the Red Cross, Sam actually felt he wouldn't make it. They would know and look forward to the particular times they went to pick up their Red Cross parcels. They were very special occasions. They were important occasions and broke up the tedium of camp life.

Day followed endless days at the camp, and the routine was always monotonously similar. As dawn would break on the Stalag all was peace and quietness. Most POWs were still dozing away or pretending to. Sam would try to tell himself that it was not morning, but a series of camp whistles would eventually tell him it wasn't so. He would wrap himself deeper into his blankets as the 'Goons' went through the camp huts and shouting "Aufstehn." The odd person he would hear was now stirring. A few men would set off to go and draw their morning brew from the cookhouse. Maybe an early riser would go for a wash in the washroom or prepare breakfast. A familiar sound was that of a spoon beating up Carnation condensed milk. Sam would often call out the much-repeated joke to his mucker, enquiring if he was chasing a mouse in the condensed milk tin this morning. Everyone would still chuckle.

Soon, the hut commander was trying to get the others on parade. This was at seven am. This process generally took quite some time, as there was no enthusiasm for it. Strange, how tired Sam felt in the mornings, given that all he had done the day before was to languish around.

Finally, all the men were up and outside for roll call, and the count began. A German officer would do this, but the compound Allied Sergeant Major would assist him. They generally tried to make these check parades quite military in style, but Sam didn't feel like a soldier anymore and, like the others, didn't really bother to stand to attention with any enthusiasm. As soon as the count was over, Sam joined the dash back to the barrack room.

Breakfast-making would start in earnest now. If Sam was feeling more energetic, he would walk up to the cookhouse and exchange his tea allowance for ready-made tea in return. This was brewed in large tubs twice a day, morning and evening. Sometimes, if he was feeling lazy or when the weather was bad, he would keep his tea and make his own brew.

Every barrack had a copper boiler in the washroom. He could get hot water there or boil it on his own blower. The blower was an ingenious invention and was a very small forge-like affair. It produced terrific heat and used little fuel. He could usually get the coal in exchange for fifty fags from a Red Cross parcel. Everyone had tea, coffee or cocoa for breakfast with black bread and jam. While he was usually enjoying his last drops of tea and a fag, laughing and joking with his mates, the Hut commander would announce that they must all get outside or on their beds so that the cleaners for the day could clean the barrack up. Keeping the Barracks clean as well as being good for discipline was absolutely vital in keeping diseases away. They took it in turn to do this unpopular chore.

"All right chaps, everybody outside and give the cleaners a chance."

Sam would make a slow attempt to get himself out of the way. Sometimes, he would just go back to bed and sleep or indulge in a book. Sometimes, he might go to school or the reference library and study. You could get a good almost university education in the school at Stalag VIIIC. Other times, he would just be a Stalag 'lazy man', hanging around outside and watching the others go walking.

When he went for a walk around the camp, he would often meet one of his friends and then stop in at the swap shops to view the stocks or trade an article from his Red Cross parcel for fags or vice versa. These swap shops were very popular and did a thriving business. No matter what he needed, it always seemed to be procurable there: any food article, any clothing article, and all types of trinkets etc. He might also note what is on at the theatre tonight. Maybe it would be a play or a band concert. Perhaps it would be his hut's turn to go this evening.

As he would pass the football ground, if there was something going on, he would stop for a few minutes and watch them practice. He was never much of a sporty type except for long walks or bike rides in the Shropshire countryside. He wondered, sometimes, how some of these guys could expend so much energy on so little food. There might be a football game that afternoon, and he could watch. Until then, Sam would wander back to the hut, as it would be nearly ten-thirty by then. Brew should soon be up, and the spuds would just about be there now anyway.

Sam would generally find one of his muckers had arrived before him and had everything well in hand. He might sit down with the spuds and peel them ready for supper. On one occasion, he had bought a package of Canadian biscuits on the stall for sixty fags, a can of butter for eighty, and jam for thirty, so a 'scoff' was the order of the day.

Sam's mucker might hand you the teapot to make a brew and also some days let you know you that they had a loaf of bread coming that afternoon. This was something to look forward to, even though the bread had a peculiar consistency. It was black bread and hard. Hard enough to kill a goon with, they used to joke. You were meant to eat in small chunks and use it to soak up any juices, which it would do completely. If anyone ate too fast or too much of it, Sam soon learned uncomfortably of the bad constipation it would give you. It contained rye but also something called wood flour and sometimes he would even straw or leaves.

After tea, he would have no more food interests except the soup, which came at noon. He generally ignored this unless it turned out to be a rare good soup. He would fill his time with a book or playing a game of bridge, which he found, to his surprise, he became quite good at.

In his tin box, Sam had a locket made of celluloid containing his sweetheart's picture. In his logbook was a colour drawing of Christine drawn by Stan from the one photo he had of her. He was quite an artist.

Even so, amid such activity, there was a very dull lazy atmosphere that gripped him in the camp. So many men and such a small percentage do anything. The biggest percentage loaf in idle meditation and reading novels or playing cards, and Sam found himself drained by it and putting off what he planned to do one day until the next.

At about four o'clock, they were summoned to supper if he hadn't been the cook himself. It might be a good one that night: bacon and egg flakes, mashed spuds, tomatoes and a big Stalag pudding - a couple of slices of black bread and jam with coffee. After supper, it would be an evening roll call, which was very similar to that of the morning. From there, if there was a show on, Sam might make a dash for it. The first there would get the better seat.

Evenings would generally be the time of visits from friends from the other parts of the camp. Some would sleep, others would read or play cards. The different sector gates were locked at eight and then would be the evening brew with maybe a small snack from his Red Cross parcel. Sam, like everyone, definitely did a lot of tea drinking. After lights out, someone might play the old gramophone, and he would go off to dreamland once more to the crackly voices of Bing Crosby or Vera Lynn.

Thus, it would end a typical day in the life of the men in Stalag VIIIC; 'The world of the living dead.'

The camp was divided into sectors by nationalities, and although kept separate by night, they could mix freely by day. All that was except the Russians. The Russians had never signed the Geneva Convention, they were told, and this gave the Germans an excuse, if they needed one, to treat them little better than animals. They were fed far less than the others and given just enough to keep them alive to carry out the worse jobs, like cleaning out the toilets and then pushing the carts full of human waste, which the Germans called 'Scheise Wagons'. This was the only time they were seen in other compounds.

Sam and all the other prisoners were appalled at the state of the skeletal figures in their midst. They would try to sneak food to them when they passed, even though this was strictly against the rules and would be harshly dealt with by the butt of the guard's rifle if caught. A few of the more sadistic guards would spit at them and trip them up. If they reacted in any way, the guard would beat them badly or sometimes even shoot them. They were treated as sub-humans by the Goons.

The stench from their sector was always in the air. It was difficult to describe, a sticky, vomit-making stench of human misery. They were never allowed to wash, and disease was rife. It was not uncommon to see men actually dying in the camp before Sam's eyes. The Russians would never report anyone as dead as they would lose that prisoner's rations. Instead, they would tie the bodies up as long as they could to stakes. The goons would never dare enter their sector for fear of disease, and so when it came to roll call, this was carried out from outside the camp, and they could not easily distinguish between the dead and the living.

This living sore in the middle of the camp just magnified Sam's feeling of misery and lack of control over his existence. It was hard to believe that anyone could live with the human misery that was the Russians' plight. And yet here he was doing just that and with absolutely nothing he could do about it. Initially, he was angry about what he saw, but gradually, like the others, he had no alternative but to accept it, but he hated himself for doing so.

After a couple of months, he finally received a letter from home. He was so relieved and briefly happy that at least someone knew he was alive. The letter was heavily censored, with any mentions of bombing or even locations deleted. He felt some of these deletions might have been justified for security reasons but many he felt were just vindictive. His mum said that they were ok and that Christine had joined the Land Army and was working in Suffolk. She heard from her now and then, but communication was difficult as the postal service was run on a shoestring. She said that Christine, in her letters, was always asking for news of him

His sense of relief and almost joy was overwhelming. He had not been forgotten. The sense that he existed was so important. The relief that Christine at least was interested in him still made his heart soar. He knew nothing was guaranteed, but he chose to believe something would happen between them in the future, and this made him smile.

"What's occurring, mate" called our Stan from the bunk below. "Good news, is it boyo?"

"Yeh, very good. At least someone knows I'm alive, and maybe my girl still loves me"

"You've kept that a bit quiet about her. Tell me some more."

"I didn't want to say too much till I knew she was alive and still interested. And she is"

"That's so tidy. You'll sleep well tonight, boy. Just don't rock the bunk too much."

Sam smiled inside and out. Even in the existence and sometimes dark misery of Stalag VIII C, a little light shone in the dark.

The next day, Sam decided he was not going to waste his time at the camp. His letters from home had made him feel he existed again, and he might have something to look forward to if he ever made it home. He decided to go along to the classes run by ex-lecturers and teachers and find out what he could do.

He could have gone to grammar school if his parents could have afforded it, and he knew he had an aptitude for learning. He was particularly interested in politics and history. Like many people, he had little knowledge of what had caused the last war and now this one or the Russian revolution. He was keen to understand more and learn what he could do to change things, if the Allies did manage to win the war, even if only a small way in the future.

Luckily there was a class being run by an ex-lecturer from Bristol University, John Mitchell. John was very happy to have him in his group, which ran a session every other day for a couple of hours. They, of course, had no textbooks and relied on John's knowledge. There were eight in the group, and he loved the discussions they had and the fact that his eyes were being opened to the complexities of all the issues and their interconnectedness. In particular, it was a revelation to him how wars started. It seemed that WWI was a war virtually no one wanted. Most of the monarchs of the countries were related in some way via Queen Victoria, and it was only in 1910 that they all attended King Edward VII's funeral. Somehow, a momentum for war had developed, and like a line of dominos, one event led to another without anyone being able to remove that one key domino that would have halted the momentum.

The end of that catastrophic war led to the winners demanding such high reparations that this war was inevitable. Sam thought about the millions that had died in that war and were dying in this just because of the egos of a few. As his ideas formed, he was determined if he ever returned home to do as much as possible as he could as an individual anyway, to make future wars at least more difficult.

As life went on in the dreary camp with all its limitations, horror and boredom, Sam gradually started to develop self-belief and self-reliance. He was determined not to let these circumstances rule his life. He would be more the master of his own destiny. He believed in a future with no wars, where he could settle down, he hoped, with Christine. He would need to survive and believe she would, too, so that they could emerge from this hell and have a wonderful life together

If only .....

Chapter 6.   The Land Army

By 1943, Britain needed more and more food as the U-boat campaign hit hard. By the end of the year, the work done by the WLA was sufficient to keep Britain in food. The WLA had provided 90,000 women to work on the land and had kept Britain in food for the duration of the war. Though Britain had rationing, no one actually starved during this time.

Some of Britain's colonies fared less well. With no food supplies from the UK, an estimated 3 million died in Britain's African colonies through malnutrition.

An estimated 2,754 civilians were killed in London by V-1 and V-2 attacks, with another 6,523 injured.

Christine wrote several letters to Sam and had a letter from him a month later to say he was now in North Africa after an unopposed seaborne landing. He wasn't looking forward to yet another seaborne landing, although it looked like he was in for one somewhere in Italy soon. She knew he hated the sea, and she smiled sympathetically as she read it.

The months she spent in London before call up she enjoyed immensely, despite the war going on around her. The family she worked for couldn't be nicer and she was able to continue at college with her qualifications. They even took her with them on a trip to the seaside on the train and it was the first time she had ever travelled first class.

Finally, in December 1942, she received a letter in the post with her call-up papers for the WLA. She was due to report to a farm at

Laxfield, East Suffolk, and it seemed she was to be given no training beforehand. She was due to report on the first day of January 1943.

In order to collect her uniform, she had to visit the WLA offices in London. She was issued with the standard outfit, which comprised of fawn cord knee breeches, some matching shirts, a green tie striped with red and bearing the letters WLA in yellow and a figure-hugging green sweater cropped at the waist. For her legs were long, thick, woollen socks, which were worn turned down over the hem of her breeches and her footwear consisted of stiff leather boots and a pair of brogues. For cold weather, she was given a fawn greatcoat, and there was also a black oilskin mac and a sou'wester. She was also given a set of coupons, which she could use to replace a limited replacement of worn garments during the year.

Unfortunately, she managed to start off on the wrong foot with the farmer she was to work for on the very first day! The porter at Liverpool Street Station mistakenly told her to change at the tenth station they stopped at, as there were no names on stations in wartime. She dozed, missed the station she was supposed to get off at and went right on to Norwich. When she anxiously arrived there, she wasn't at first sure what to do. She asked the station master if there was a local WLA office, and to her relief, he gave her directions and said it was nearby. They were very understanding when she turned up there, and they phoned the farmer. Catching the next train back, she eventually arrived there at teatime.

Mr Piper, the farmer, was none too pleased to have to go to the station twice in one day.

"Twice I bin 'ere today. Ope, this isn't what it's goin to be like with you," he said by way of welcome.

He was about fifty, lean and scrawny and had a face that always looked like it had just received bad news. He obviously wasn't convinced about the idea of the WLA but had little choice given the shortage of men. He had two farms, one on each side of the village of Laxfield. She was to be based at Green House Farm and lived with Mr and Mrs Woodborough, the tenant farmers there and their young daughter, Ada. Her room was small but acceptable. There was a jug of water and a metal bowl, underneath the bed was a chamber pot that she was soon to realise was her responsibility to empty and clean every day.

She was woken at six am, and her first job that morning was to go into a yard with about twenty bullocks and bed them down with fresh straw. When she asked for a little more detail, the farmer said, "You'll soon get the 'ang of it," with a slight grin.

With little idea of what this involved she soon realised this was a test set for her. It was somewhat of a shock to a city girl like Christine after just arriving from London. She was determined somehow to show them and do it. The bullocks were frisky and would push into her. She found by accident that a quick slap on the nose made them retreat, and she could get on with her work.

She soon learned how labour-intensive farm work was. There was little in the way of any machinery, and even tractors were a rarity, it seemed. She had arrived just in time for the sugar beet harvest, which she later realised was the hardest task of the year. It was a bitterly cold job, chopping off the green tops with sharp choppers and then loading them onto trailers. From there, they were taken to the railway station and then onto trucks to be processed at the Factory. Although it was hard work, Christine felt good that at least she was helping to supply the nation's sugar.

It was mainly fieldwork, though the Pipers had a herd of bullocks and a flock of sheep. Once, Christine got soaked from chasing sheep out of a field of Kale. She and another girl, Jean, had been sent to keep them out of it and just make them graze on a clover overlay field of stubble. It was an impossible task!

They also did a lot of potato picking and putting them into 'clamps.' Another extremely freezing job was riddling potatoes in winter. The 'Riddler' was a manually worked machine for grading the size of potatoes. Jean fed the potatoes into a circular wire cage at one end, and then Christine turned the handle. Small ones dropped through what were called 'chats' and were then fed to animals. Although it was hard work, Christine still had a job to keep the cold from seeping into her bones.

She would prepare a bottle of tea and sandwiches before she left in the morning, and these and the then cold tea would often have to last her until teatime. No matter what the weather she was never invited into the house during the day. If near enough she would eat in the barn or the stable, otherwise in the fields. She had been allocated one week's holiday a year and used it by dividing it between Christmas and whenever Mr Piper could spare her in Summer. Bank holidays, though gave her the chance to have a weekend in London.

She developed a great friendship with Peggy, who worked on a neighbouring farm. She lived in Ipswich, a lucky girl. Christine used to go home with her sometimes and her Mum very kindly let her have a real bath. At the farm, she could only have a wash down in the bedroom, nearly always with cold water.

She surprised herself with how she adapted to these conditions, and surprisingly, despite these deprivations she actually found she enjoyed the work and the life. She felt she had a purpose in life and found that her spirit and sense of fun and friendliness shone through.

Soon, the Americans started arriving in the area, and Suffolk and Norfolk being quite flat they soon built airfields all around them. Their Flying Fortresses were huge bombers, and they used to fly around and around in the early morning, getting into formation for the daylight bombing raids over Germany. She used to watch them coming home in the afternoon, and she could often see that some were badly damaged.

One afternoon, while working in the fields, she looked up, her attention being grabbed by a spluttering engine rather than the usual throbbing droning sound of an American bomber engine. The plane was in trouble, she could see, as smoke was billowing from one of the engines. It sank lower and lower, and Christine watched on with her heart in her mouth, praying that it would reach the runway. It dipped out of sight, and for a brief hopeful moment, it looked like it had when suddenly there was a loud explosion, and a ball of smoke and flame rose into the air in the direction of the runway. She realised the worst had happened, and it broke her heart to think of those fine young men having survived a dangerous mission, then having lives being wasted like that at the last. It again made her think about Sam and what he must be going through. She missed him so much and wondered whether they would ever somehow meet again.

On weekend evenings, she and Peggy would go to the local village dances, and although they were short of male dancing partners, they would dance together and enjoy the evenings. There were several dances that did not require a partner anyway. One of these dances was the 'Lambeth Walk'. Another popular dance in the first year of the war was one developed from 'The Siegfried Line', where all the dancers simulated doing their washing and hanging it out on the Siegfried Line. Two other relatively simple dances were; 'The Chestnut Tree' and 'Knees Up Mother Brown'. These involved some singing as well as dancing and were always great fun. Whenever these tunes would start up, the dance floors would soon be packed, with everyone doing the same dance.

They were also provided with WLA bicycles, very heavy cumbersome things, and she and Peggy twice cycled the seven miles to the Anglo-American club at Framlingham. The bands were fabulous. Often, their singers would be handsome, tall black men. While she had seen black men occasionally before, never as glamorous as this. They had only occasionally heard music like this on the radio. Some of the Americans were absolutely amazing dancers to the new music. Christine was a reasonable dancer and could waltz and foxtrot, but this was something else. The American 'Boogie-Woogie' had a pulsating beat, which just invited everyone to dance! The Yanks would dance the 'Jitterbug' to it, and some of their moves, throwing their partner in the air or between their legs, were wonderful and hugely exhilarating.

The first time Christine saw the Yanks, she thought they were all officers; their uniforms were smart, and they wore collars and ties so different to our soldiers in their rough khaki uniforms. They were like film stars and had badges for everything. They would say,

"Gee honey, this one is for sharpshooting", and so on. The locals would say, probably a little jealously, "They get a medal for the one who can spit furthest." One Christine met came from Chicago, and he said:

"Honey, when I get back, I'm going to be mayor of Chicago".

They liked girls and were polite, and would say to Christine, "Honey, you look like a million dollars in that dress" or "Baby, when this war is over, I'm taking you back to the States".

Christine and her friends would take it all with a pinch of salt. The Yanks did, though, brighten everyone's lives, she thought. They brought tins of food: Hershey chocolate bars, salted peanuts and lovely cakes.

It was a chance to get away from the farm and the greyness and worry of war, although Mr Piper did not like Christine going out in the evening, as he thought she would be too tired to work hard the next day. This never stopped them. Anyway, Christine felt he was pretty ungrateful, given how hard she worked.

On her way home one clear and cloudless night, she glanced up at the sky above her. There, right in front of her, was the constellation of Orion the Hunter that Sam had helped her recognise. And shining brightly with its reddish hue was Beetlejuice, Orion's armpit. She stopped and gazed up at it wondering if Sam might be doing the same things at that moment. It was unlikely, of course, but she hoped it was so.

As she was visiting the town near the airbase the following day, a black American serviceman came up to ask her the way to the newsagents. She didn't know the answer immediately and shook her head as she thought about it.

"I'm sorry, I'm afraid I don't know," she said.

He obviously believed that what she was saying was that she wouldn't help him because he was black, as he quickly said

"I'm really sorry, Ma'am that I stopped you in the street. I really hope I haven't made any trouble for you."

And with that, he hurried off. Christine felt terrible, and the thought that she had innocently hurt someone that much really troubled her. She hadn't even considered his colour, but it seemed that in the USA, that was still a major issue. We are all fighting together in a war, she thought. How could people on the same side anyway treat others like that? Especially when at the dances when they were singing, they were admired by all.

She was constantly anxious about Sam, and to write to him or send parcels meant that she had to have a special type of letter to write to POWs that she had to get from the Post Office. She couldn't write that much, and it was heavily censored. They wrote to each other for a while, but after D-Day, things began to get worse, and nothing seemed to get through in the end.

Early in June, she listened to the radio announcing that the Germans had started a new bombing attack on London by sending over pilotless V-1 flying bombs. They apparently looked like small planes with flames coming from the back. For a while, this had been kept in the dark, and people did not know what they were. Her Mum and Dad did not talk about this for some time in their letters because, as she found out later, they didn't want to worry her.

In early May, a telegram arrived for her. Telegrams rarely brought good news, and she opened it with dread. She read it with a mixture of shock and relief. It said that their house had been virtually destroyed by a flying bomb. They were both safe as they had been out visiting friends at the time. A great friend of her mums, Mrs Farmer, had taken them in for the time being, and they were safe and well.

They implored her not to come home as her life might be in danger from these weapons. She insisted, and the grumpy Mr Piper reluctantly gave her the weekend off, and she went home. She first went to her old home, and when she saw what was left of it, she was shocked and saddened. Tears welled up as she took in the wrecked remains of her childhood home. After a while, she dragged herself away and made her way to the Farmers' house to see her parents.

When she arrived at Mrs Farmer's, her parents were very calm about things and she thought incredibly brave, considering what they had been through. She implored them to go away to the countryside, at least for a while, but they wouldn't. Her Dad said he had to work, and the chances of being hit again were remote, he joked.

Reluctantly and tearfully, she caught the train back on Sunday afternoon. Her mum hugged her and waved her off from the front gate, and her Dad came with her to Liverpool Street Station. He hugged her and put a pound note into her hand as he squeezed it. As the train moved away, they waved to each other until they were out of sight. She prayed every day for their safety, and always in her heart, she really thought they were indestructible. She felt they were the best parents anyone could have, and she missed them so much. It was, though, to be the last time she ever saw them alive.

Then came that calamitous day that would stay embedded in her memory forever. She was hoeing in the sugar beet field when she saw Mrs Piper walking towards her. She soon realised from her face that something was wrong. She walked up to Christine, and unusually for her, as she rarely displayed much emotion, she put her arms around Christine and hugged her. As she drew away, she said with tears rolling down her face, "We have had a telegram.

Your mum and dad have been killed by a German bomb" "No, it can't be; that just can't be. They were bombed but survived it. You've got it wrong. You must have."

"No, my dear, this is another bomb. I am so, so, sorry."

Christine let out an almost unearthly wail and all but collapsed into Mrs Piper's arms.

"Come on, my dear. Let's get you back to the farmhouse."

Christine walked and stumbled across the muddy field in a complete daze. The news just wouldn't sink in. They were indestructible, weren't they? Perhaps they hadn't found them yet in the rubble. Her head said they would be ok, she knew they would be, but her heart was telling her something else. They arrived at the farmhouse, and Mrs Piper sat her down at the table and brought her a cup of tea and a hanky. She then showed her the telegram.

"We regret to inform you that Mr & Mrs Harold and Jane Tucker were killed on 23rd June by a German Flying bomb."

There was no mistaking the terse and awful words. Now, the tears came thick and fast, and she just sobbed and sobbed. The Pipers, after all their sternness and seemingly unfriendliness, now revealed a different side to their character. They were warm and supportive and made sure she was looked after. Unable to go to London that night as she had missed the last train and eventually worn out by the grief, she went to bed exhausted. Mr Piper had said he knew the times of the trains and would be there to take her to the station the next morning. She was not to worry about anything, and they would be able to look after everything until she was ready to come back.

She didn't know how she travelled to London the next day. Everything passed in a blur. Her cousin Doris was there to meet her as a result of the telegram she had managed to send to her mum's sister, her Aunty Janice. Doris gave her a huge, tearful hug and helped her with her bags as they negotiated the underground. Elsie was already at Mrs Farmers, and when they met, they just hugged each other tightly and sobbed their hearts out.

The next day, they went to see their Aunt Flo, her mum's cousin, in hospital. She had been in the same room as her Mum and Dad but had survived the blast. The nurse told them they shouldn't stay long as she was still very weak. Aunty Flo looked terrible and had injuries that would obviously keep her in hospital for some time. Aunty Flo told them some of the sad stories.

"We were having for lunch, chips and dried egg omelette. You know, the dried egg that comes in waxed packets from America. Anyway, I was peeling potatoes at the sink, and mum was at the stove on the opposite side of the room cooking this egg omelette and chips. Anyway, the next thing I knew, this was about midday. The next thing I knew was, I sort of heard something and thought, 'Oh, someone's getting it!' But in that split second, everything fell in. The kitchen had a middle door to the yard, the top half of which was glass, and two windows on either side of that. All the glass and the windows and the door flew in, but unluckily, your Mum was on one side of the room with your Dad, and I was on the other and ...." she sobbed, "so I survived and, and, your Mum & Dad didn't."

This was the randomness of a war that chose its victims arbitrarily. She managed to give them a tearful smile but that was all she managed when they left.

Elsie told Christine the full story, as she had arrived a day earlier than Christine and had gleaned everything from the family. Apparently, after staying a while at their friends, the Farmers, Christine's parents had moved to live with Mrs Jennings, a friend of Mrs Farmer who had self-contained rooms to spare in their house. They had moved there just two days before the bomb fell. Mrs Jennings had been sitting on a sofa with her daughter-in-law and her dog in the drawing room. This was above the kitchen where Mum, Dad and Aunty Flo were. Mrs Jennings was blown into the garden, sustaining a broken leg, while her daughter-in-law and the dog were killed. Life was just so random she reflected again sadly.

Her Aunt Janice and her husband Uncle John and family were marvellous, coping with everything for them. They arranged the funeral, and it must have been awful for them, too. A service was held for her Mum and Dad at Holy Trinity Church, and then this was followed by a burial at Finchley Cemetery. Her parents were very popular and many of her mum's Mother's Union and Church members, and also some of the men from her Dad's workplace, Lilley and Skinner, attended. A few days later, her Dad's boss invited Elsie and Christine to the firm's premises, where they showed them where her Dad had worked. He told them what a big loss he was to the firm. They also presented them with a sum of money they had collected. The girls tearfully thanked them.

They had another sad time a few days later when accompanied by Aunt Janice, they sold off the few items from their home that had been salvaged. Christine would have liked to keep some of the things, but there was absolutely nowhere to store anything.

As if things could get no worse, unfortunately they did. A few days after the funeral she received a letter from Sam's mum. It said he was missing in action from the landings at Anzio. She was now an absolute wreck, and it was only her sister's support that probably stopped her from having a complete breakdown. She eventually lay on her bed and sobbed herself to sleep, emotionally exhausted.

When she awoke the next morning, her sister soon arrived with a cup of tea

She said, "I've been thinking, Chrissy, you must not go back to Suffolk. I need you, and you need me to help us get through this."

She insisted that they should visit the WLA welfare officer to see if Christine could be transferred to join Elsie in South Wales. They arranged this the next day, and the very understanding Welfare Officer, with a few phone calls, made everything happen.

Christine was to go to South Wales with Elsie and be with her at her hostel where she would have plenty of sympathetic female help around her.

With the dreaded flying bombs still falling, Elsie and Christine had an awful scare themselves while still in London. Out one day walking, they sensed suddenly as they heard first the distant hum and then the louder harsh rattle of a V1 flying bomb. If the noise wasn't coming from the sky, it would have sounded like a noisy diesel lorry engine revving very fast. They looked up and spotted the small, almost bird-like object, and then followed it with their eyes until it reached the space in the sky above where they were standing. They held their breath; if the engine stopped before it got to them, they knew that was the time to really worry.

It was just about overhead when the noise stopped abruptly. They counted down the twelve seconds of silence, as they had been told to, from the engine cutting out before there would be the blast of the explosion. They waited in tense, terrifying trepidation, closing their eyes and holding each other closely. Christine just couldn't believe that they, too, might suffer the same fate as their parents. The same terrifying thought must have flashed through the minds of everyone who heard that flying bomb at that moment: go silent. Are these few seconds my last? Sadly, for someone, it would be, but luckily, for the two sisters at least, the explosion that followed was about half a mile away.

They couldn't wait to get out of London and were looking forward to catching the train to Newport the next day. They arrived in Newport mid-afternoon and caught the bus to St Mellons, where the Land Army hostel was. The girls there were very warm and friendly, and Annie, who managed the Hostel and was referred to by all the girls as Aunty Annie, was a delight and reminded her so much of her mum.

Several weeks later, she received another letter from Sam's mother to say that he was alive and a prisoner of the Germans. However, she was hugely relieved that relief for her was countered by her worry for him. He must be been going through absolute hell she thought.

That night, the sky was clear, and in the blackout, the stars were out in all their splendour. Christine looked up and sought out the three stars which made up the belt of the constellation of Orion the Hunter, and as she moved her eyes upwards, there glowing with a red hue was Orion's armpit, Beetlejuice. She wondered if Sam could be seeing the same thing. She hoped he would be and remembered that night in Shropshire and that at least brought her some comfort.

Chapter 7. The Long March

In January 1945, as the Soviet army was advancing through Poland towards Germany, the Nazis made the decision to evacuate the POW camps to prevent the liberation of the prisoners by the Russians. In fact, it was more to do with the Germans using POW's as a shield. About 30,000 Allied POWs were force-marched westward across Poland and Germany in groups of 200 to 300 in appalling winter conditions, lasting about four months from January to April 1945. It has been called various names: 'The Great March West', 'The Long March', 'The Long Walk', 'The Long Trek', 'The Black March' and 'The Bread March', but most survivors just called it 'The March.' Many of them died from the bitter cold and exhaustion.

During this period, also hundreds of thousands of German civilians, most of them women and children, as well as civilians of other nationalities, were making their way westward in the snow and freezing weather and many died. January and February 1945 were among the coldest winter months of the twentieth century, with blizzards and temperatures as low as -25°C; even until the middle of March, temperatures were well below -18 °C. Most of the POWs were ill-prepared for the evacuation, having suffered months of poor rations and wearing clothing ill-suited to the appalling winter conditions.

The prisoners in Sam's hut gathered around their secret radio, which was strong enough to pick up the BBC news. It was the best source of news. Their radio had been constructed from smuggled parts by two RAF ground technicians, who, with amazing bad luck in their only airborne test exercise, had been shot down over Holland. It first operated on the camp electrical system, but it was later converted to run on batteries so that they could listen to the BBC nightly broadcast when the camp electricity supply had been cut off. The receiver was concealed within a wall panel located behind a bed in the hut, some of the fixing nails acting as terminals to which an aerial wire and earphone cables could be attached. Only two almost invisible points on the wall disclosed where the radio was erected. When someone joined these points by a short length of wire, the set was automatically switched on to the correct wavelength and the wonderful chimes of London's Big Ben preceded the nightly news.

There were also designated listeners who transcribed the news onto pieces of toilet paper. This paper was then hidden in a tin of dried milk that had been fitted with a false bottom. After roll call the next morning, the notes were dictated to a typist who made a copy on a small, very thin sheet of paper. This paper was then folded and hidden in a hollow wristwatch worn by Sergeant Roger Drummond, who then circulated the news around the camp. Although he was often searched, this paper was never discovered.

They were starting to pick up more and more information, and the news was generally encouraging. The Allies were advancing from the west, albeit with a few setbacks, and the Russians were making much swifter progress from the east. The signs were that the end of their miserable captivity might be in sight. The radio was stowed away and the mood of the hut after the broadcast was positive that night, as the men got themselves ready for sleep.

Although conditions were getting worse and the weather was relentlessly, bitterly and numbingly cold, the mood of the prisoners was, by contrast, becoming warmer and more upbeat. The news from all fronts in the war had indicated that the Nazis were at last on the run and that the liberation of their camp was in sight, and with an end, they prayed to their misery. The message to be delivered from the two British officers who entered the hut at that moment was to change all that. The fact that they were also accompanied by three German officers was an indication in itself that something serious was about to be announced.

Captain Harry Llewelyn called the men together and then said in his lilting Welsh accent, "Boys, I'm sorry to tell you this, but we have to move out at seven am tomorrow. We have been told this is for our own safety to ensure we are supposedly out of any direct fighting in line with the Geneva Convention. I have to tell you, though, that I think the bastards' motives are far more devious."

One of the German officers looked up sharply at this but Captain Llewelyn ignored the gaze carried on.

"I'm not sure how far we'll have to walk, they say only a few days. There is no easy way to say this. We are short of food and the right clothing for this dreadful weather, but we must somehow make the most of it. Do whatever you can to make your clothing as warm as possible. Look after your boots especially. If you have any extra socks, layers of paper or even dry grass, stuff them in your boots to keep your feet from freezing. God knows how far we will have to walk - they have been very vague about this. It goes without saying you should get together any rations you can."

The captain looked slowly around at the glum and worried faces and took in the sombre mood. He responded by raising his voice and shouting out.

"Come on, lads, we have survived a lot so far. We're not going to let these bastards beat us now, are we?"

A cheer, along with a number of other expletives about the Nazis, resounded around the hut.

"They are short of guards, so we have been ordered to get into groups of about two hundred and fifty, and we will have about ten guards with each group," he continued after the noise had died down. "We have organised the groups, and the names are on this list."

He showed them a sheet of paper.

"Each group will be allocated at least one officer and one NCO of ours. Bring any food you can carry and go to the Red Cross hut for more. We have been told that there will be further supplies on the road from the dear old Red Cross. The Nazis are supposed to feed us, too," he smiled sarcastically, "but doubtless, we will have to live as best we can off the land as well. Remember it's their duty to find shelter for us at night, but I suspect we won't be the only ones on the road, and we will have to look for shelter where we can. Any questions?"

Apart from more grumbles and curses, there were none. What could they do anyway? They all had become accustomed to setbacks, ill-treatment and challenges. They didn't blame many of their prison guards, as they looked as forlorn and worried as them. As the war dragged on, the camp had been left with older and older guards, as anyone else was needed at the front. Many of these had sons and daughters who were involved in the conflict, and they shared their worries with the prisoners from time to time. A few sadistic bastards were still left, though, and most prisoners vowed silently to pay them back for their cruelty if the opportunity ever arose.

Sam with all the others, crammed around the list that the Captain had stuck on the wall. He was relieved, at least to see he was with his mates. He had regained much of the weight he had lost en route to the camp with dysentery, mainly due to Red Cross parcels and the kindness of the medical team, who had managed to keep him in the hospital much longer than they were supposed to. Although clothes no longer hung on him, he was far from fully fit and was feeling apprehensive about his ability to survive long on a march in these freezing winter conditions.

Mick, one of his 'muckers', who had especially taken him under his wing since he moved into the hut, noticed this and said kindly.

"It'll be ok, lad, stick with me, and we'll get through this. We mustn't let the Nazi feckers win."

Sam smiled weakly and nodded in reply. He was always slightly amused at the Irish swear word.

"Thanks, Mick, let's bloody hope so. And at least we are walking in the right direction - towards home," he smiled.

But would he ever get home, wondered Sam? Every time positive news seemed about to ignite the flames of freedom, something happened to dampen the hopeful embers. However, despite these gloomy thoughts, he also felt growing within him a mental strength. Despite his experiences so far, or maybe because of them, he found he was developing a certain resilience. This current challenge reminded him of the ordeals he had endured so far just getting to this camp from Italy and that he had indeed survived life-threatening conditions on the way. That in itself was an accomplishment. And it brought to mind something else, too. It reminded him that the damage war had inflicted on him had, in many ways, left him stronger. What had hurt him in the past, he realised, would actually make him better equipped to face the present. He was no longer the innocent country boy. In that moment of realisation, he felt the re-awakening of a determination and a resolution to survive. At that moment, he knew he would get through this. He would see Christine. He would see his family once again. He would, he would, he would.

During the next few hours, with renewed energy, Sam spent his time cutting up blankets to make extra linings for the inside of his clothes and boots and hoods to add to the balaclava he had received from the Red Cross. Where there weren't enough blankets, he stuffed paper, cardboard and straw inside his clothes. At least his baggy clothes helped him now, he thought. Sam and his two muckers made a visit to the Red Cross hut and were allocated as much food as was available.

At exactly seven the next morning, the ever-punctual guards burst into the huts, banging on the bunks, shouting unenthusiastically "Raus, Raus!" Sam, like all of the men, had not undressed that night in preparation for the next day's ordeal. They had shredded most of the blankets the previous evening, and besides, it was always cold in the hut, as the stove would inevitably die out during the night.

They all slowly crawled from their bunks. Someone restarted the stove, and they made themselves a drink of warm, weak tea from tea leaves now being used for at least the second time. Still, it was better than nothing.

Sam, with the others emerged from the hut and organised himself into his marching group. It was numbingly cold, and his breath literally froze in the air. The guards carried out the daily roll call, and there was an unusual reluctance from the men to carry out their usual pranks to confuse and irritate the Germans. It was too cold for that, thought Sam, and if they had to go, he, like all the others, just wanted to get going. He stamped around to keep warm, and before long, they were ordered to start marching off in their separate groups.

The different groups started off together, but soon, they were directed away from each other as much as possible to give the guards a degree of control. Not that anyone was considering escape particularly, thought Sam. They were in the middle of bloody Germany, where could he or anyone else go? If they went east towards the Russians moving towards them, they could be caught up in the fighting. Besides, if they were to be released, it would be so much better if this was to the Yanks or the British. The very nature of the countryside and tracks also ensured that they had to separate in order to keep moving. It also spread them out, which, to be fair, gave them a better chance of finding other food and shelter, he thought.

Before long, he realised that they were not the only people on the move. There was a continuous trickle of refugees fleeing west. In the camp, there had been rumours and stories of how the Russians had been retaliating against not only the German army but ordinary people as well. He could see these German refugees knew the treatment they would expect if captured by the Russians, especially the women, and the fear showed in their faces. He knew he could do nothing to help, and he avoided making eye contact with the prisoners and plodded on with his eyes cast down in misery.

The ground was flat and frozen, as were the streams and any water they came across. Sam wondered how they would get water without heat to melt the ice. He plodded on with Mick by his side, occasionally sharing encouraging glances. It was too cold to talk much.

By midday, at least the sun had come out. Even though the warmth it brought was feeble, it was better than nothing. At least they had escaped the smell of death and decay in the camp, especially that emanating from the Russian sector. The fresh air even if freezing, gave them all a boost. They stopped for a rest and found a few fallen trees to sit on rather than the frozen ground. There was nowhere obvious for the men to relieve themselves, and they could see from scattered stinking puddles they were not the first on this journey.

Sam and Mick shared a tin of very cold but not quite frozen, spam.

"What a bloody mess," said Mick. "Let's hope we can find some bleedin' shelter tonight, though it looks like we will have a lot of feckin competition."

They surveyed the almost dystopian scene. The refugees consisted mainly of older men, women and younger children. Everyone else had been forced into the fighting. They seemed to be mostly German peasants, but mixed in were the skeletal forms of others who had obviously been the subjects of forced labour and very meagre rations. A number of them wore a kind of stripped clothing, why he could not guess then. Some had handcarts with their meagre belongings piled into them. The women wearily carried the younger children. In any other situation, the men would have offered to help. The instinct of self-survival, though, had driven out most feelings of empathy.

Wearily, the guards stood up and started to urge the men to march on again. One or two resisted, but a few sharp thumps with rifle butts from the more sadistic ones did the trick, and soon they were on the move again. The weak sun, unable to provide enough warmth, gave up its battle with the encroaching mist and gradually faded away behind it. They marched on and on and on.

By late afternoon, they had covered about twelve miles, although, to Sam, it felt a lot more. They were all weary and started to look around for possible shelter before the winter night closed in. Their NCO spotted a group of about fifty of what appeared to be pig sheds ahead. The pigs, he realized unsurprisingly, had vanished. Most things edible seemed to have gone the same way. He shouted to the guards to make them understand that they could be shelter for the night, and the guards soon understood and they self-organised themselves into the sheds. The sheds were only small and could fit in about ten tightly packed men. They stank of pig muck, though luckily, it was frozen. Anyway, his sense of what smelt bad was diminishing in line with the worsening of his own personal hygiene.

The leader of their group, Sergeant Brian Elder, arrived at Sam's hut on his rounds of the sheds, checking out the state of the men.

"You ok, lads?" He asked. "What a shit day," he continued. "Remember now to look after your feet. Don't take your boots off, no matter how much they hurt, because you might not get them on again. Each hut must organise a scouting party to look for wood and whether there is any food around. Not that it's very likely. I know it's a bit of a squash in there, but that's a good thing because it will help keep you a little warmer, and I won't tell," he said with a wink. "You can relieve yourselves in the bushes in the far left of the field. Let's try and act like bloody humans, at least in that regard."

With that, he left and moved on to the next shed.

Sam and Mick went to look for any wood they could find. And they followed the other men towards a wooded area about a few hundred yards away. There were twigs, brush and branches lying around, and they pulled together a pile and tied it up so that they could drag it back.

"Some of this will be useful to block the front of our stinking shed from the cold, at least," said Mick.

As they dragged their bundle back to the hut, Sam thought of home and, of course, of Christine. One letter from his mother had got through before he left, which, because of censorship, gave little news of her or Christine. He wondered if he would ever see her again. It was the main thing that kept him going. While he walked, he had constructed a future fantasy world in his head. They had settled in a small cottage in the countryside and he had a good steady job. A couple of kids would be playing in the garden, and some chickens would be keeping the weeds down.

"Where are you?" remarked Mick.

"Miles and miles and miles away," smiled Sam weakly, "dreaming of home."

"We'll get there, lad. Might not seem that way at the moment, but we'll get there. I have to see my family again. I just feckin fekin have to. And if I'm going to, I'll damn well make sure you get to see yours too, Sammy boy."

"Thanks, Mick. Not sure what I'd do without my muckers," replied Sam as they trudged on towards the hut.

Amazingly, they soon had turned the hut into something almost habitable, and with a fire going, their spirits rose slightly. While the war often brought the worst out of people it could also bring the best. Acts of kindness and self-sacrifice between the POWs were commonplace. Creativity abounded both in making the best of things but also in entertaining themselves and keeping their spirits up. Some of the men wrote poetry and read these out. Some told stories - some true, some made up. Sam told them of his escape from the frozen pond when he was young.

"Might be a useful skill out here, Sam," chuckled one of the men when he had finished. Some found new words to familiar songs that they sang at night and when they marched. No one could blame them for the earthiness of the lyrics, given the grimness of the situation. They even scratched a name on their hut: 'The Night Sty.' Eventually, despite the cold, the sour smell of pig muck, and sweaty men huddled together, weariness took over, and all of them fell fitfully asleep.

The next morning, just before dawn, he awoke gradually and was soon fully awakened by a dawn chorus of expletives, insults and bodily noises. Once one man was up, given the space, as a result, everyone was brought to a drowsy consciousness and a realisation of where they were and again how bloody cold it was. They slowly organised themselves. Sam helped light a fire while others went off to visit the far corner of the field. Breakfast consisted of an oat and rye black porridge that had become a staple during their time in capture.

Soon, the German guards arrived. They looked decidedly fresher. It turned out they had been given, or more likely taken, space at a nearby cottage and, as a result, fed well. They were quite happy to point this out to the men, and one of them, whom they called 'Scarface,' for the obvious reason of a long red and purple scar that ran down the side of his face, couldn't keep himself from kicking over their pot of boiling water saying with a smirk "Enschuldigen sie bitte."

"I'll get that Nazi fucker one of these days, just you see," whispered Stan. "Just see if I don't."

On the afternoon of the third day, as Sam and the others were moving wearily along an open road, he became aware of the drone of an aircraft engine gradually becoming louder. He knew this was unlikely to be a German plane as their once proud and huge air force, they had heard on the radio, had largely been beaten into a shadow of its former glory. He nudged Mick, who was, as usual, walking next to him.

"Can you hear that plane? I reckon it must be one of ours?"

They both looked up, scanning the clear blue sky, and he saw a plane coming towards them and could just make out RAF colours. They shouted to the others and pointed at it and everyone started shouting and waving frantically and excitedly at the plane as it came closer and closer. The plane, a Spitfire, someone shouted, swooped lower and lower towards them, as if to give a greeting fly by.

Suddenly, their excitement was crushed as all hell let loose as the plane opened fire on them. Everyone dived frantically for the cover of the roadside ditches. No sooner had Sam dived for cover and recovered to look up than he saw that it was coming in for another pass, and the firing started again. The ground became alive with bullets all around them, and he flung himself down and stayed there until they were sure the plane had vanished.

"What the feck," shouted Mick, getting to his feet. "You alright, lad."

Sam was badly shaken but not injured. He surveyed the scene. Amazingly, there seemed to be few casualties. A guard lay obviously dead on the road along with two prisoners. Cries of pain from the ditches on the other side of the road suggested at least one or two had been hit and injured, too.

"The maniac must have thought we were bloody Germans!" exclaimed Sam. "Couldn't they bloody well see, the stupid idiots! That's the second time they have tried to get me." And then he laughed at the absurdity of that.

Brian Elder appeared, "You alright down there?" They nodded.

"We have three injured over the other side, but not badly. We were bloody lucky, that's for sure. Bleedin' blind, bastard RAF, idiot."

They were all badly shaken. It was bad enough with the Germans and the weather trying to kill them off! From then on, they were all naturally more wary, and as they started off again, Sam surveyed the sky with a wary vigilance.

A few of the villages they passed through were hostile, sometimes just passively by locking themselves away and not responding to the shouting and banging on their doors. Sometimes, they were openly more hostile, hurling stones and insults at them. The guards, it seemed, were generally not in the mood to force the

119

issue against any resistance, and they passed through as speedily as they could.

This was not by any means always the case. A number of villages were very welcoming, providing them with food and proper shelter. This was amazing in itself, given the poor conditions they were in themselves. One night, a farmer and his family put Sam and a number of his group up in a barn on the straw and fed them a warm, weak vegetable stew and even some boiled eggs in the morning!

As the days wore on, though, Sam, despite his will to survive, realised he was becoming increasingly weaker and, although determined, was finding it difficult to keep up the pace. Although it had been six months since his earlier ordeal from Italy to eastern Germany, a POW camp was by no means somewhere to recover completely, and it had left him with little body fat to call on. His poor diet and the dysentery that he had suffered meant that wounds and sores seemed to take longer to heal. He had blisters on his feet he dared not look at, and the cold sores on his legs looked dreadful.

They usually walked up to sixteen miles a day, and although they often found somewhere to sleep under cover at night, the cumulative effect of long walks in the cold and the absence of real warmth started to take effect on many. They had already had a few fatalities, and the German guards, keen to get as far away from the advancing Russians as they could, were generally unsympathetic to those who couldn't keep up. Sam was determined not to let his weakness show.

Sometimes, he was allowed to sit on one of the few hand-drawn carts for a while. He was he knew, along with a number of others, reaching the end of his resources. He knew the blisters on his feet and chilblains on his legs were getting worse and very sore, even though he dared not remove anything to check because of the bitter cold. Sergeant Elder was very concerned about him and a number of others and Mick had urged him to see if anything could be done.

On the ninth day, the Germans, partly out of a growing panic that the Russians were getting ever closer and that injured and weak men were slowing them down, said that those who could not carry on much further would be left at another huge POW camp, Stalag IVB. They said they had apparently received orders that they could do this, though no one could see how. They were due to pass within ten miles of the camp the next day. It was not to be evacuated yet mainly due to the sheer numbers of POWs there, their mixed nationalities, including many Russians, and the lack of guards to escort them.

Twenty-three of the men were singled out by the guards, and with the careful oversight of Brian Elder, Sam was included to be taken off to the camp. The rest were told they would need to walk on for at least another eighty miles to the southwest, somewhere near the Austrian border. Mick made his farewells to Sam and they hugged each other and promised to get in touch again when they could after the war.

Sam was concerned that once out of sight, they might be abandoned by the guards or possibly worse. He said so to Brian Elder, who then walked up to the two guards that were due to escort them and shouted right in their faces.

"You had better make sure they get there. If when this is all over, I find out they haven't, I'm coming back for you, and you can't even imagine what I'll do to you."

It was an empty threat, of course, partly because they couldn't understand him and partly because it would likely be impossible to carry out. But the sheer force of his words and personality seemed to have an effect, and Sam and the others felt marginally safer as a result.

Brian said quietly to him, "Keep an eye on them. I think you're ok with Baldy, but not so sure about the other bastard. I'm relying on you, Sam, to get them all there safely."

"I will do my best. And thanks for all your support. You have a bloody tough march ahead, too. Good luck."

"And all the best to you, Sam, you've done well."

With that, they moved off in their separate ways. Sam did keep his eye on the guards and worked out contingency plans of action in his head. He was beginning to notice, even in his sorry state, that not only Brian Elder but also the others in this group were starting to look to him for decisions. As they walked on and on, he denied the weariness that dragged upon their spirits like leaden weights and enthused the others to keep going.

He didn't remember much of the rest of the march. He counted steps to keep going. He thought of Christine. He looked up at the sky and made out Beetlejuice. He tried every strategy he knew to take his mind off the cold, the pain and the weariness.

Suddenly, it was over. Five hours later, twenty of the twenty-three men, escorted by one guard, staggered into the Stalag. Three of their group had collapsed on the way. They all died in a similar fashion. After collapsing, they became delirious and didn't know where they were. Even though it was very cold they even tried to rip their clothes off. They tried all ways to save them, including actually lying to them to stop this and talking to them and encouraging them as much as they could. However, they seemed to quickly pass away where they fell. It was as if once their bodies gave in, their minds simply decided to call it a day. There was no alternative but to somehow just keep walking step after step after step after step.

They sadly took their identification tags from those they left behind, and also any personal items, determined to ensure that their loved ones would know what happened rather than receive the anonymous missing-in-action telegram. The ground was too hard, and they were too tired anyway to bury them. They had no choice but to just leave them and carry on.

They had started out with two guards, but one had suddenly disappeared into and then reappeared from, a house they passed on the way, now dressed in civilian clothes. After a short argument with the other guard, he disappeared into the countryside. The remaining guard could have left them, too. This would have put them at even greater risk as they might have been seen as escapees. The guard, a man in his early sixties, Sam guessed, was a decent man, they knew and took his responsibilities seriously even if there was this apparent route to safety for him.

The prisoners in the camp welcomed them, and some of his group were taken straight to the hospital, while others, including Sam, went through the dreadful disinfecting regime again before being allocated to a hut. His sores stung viciously in the shower and didn't look at all good. Still, with the addition of disinfecting powder and some bandages, he hoped they would not be getting worse.

It still felt like heaven to Sam to be in a simple POW hut, and although it was still cold inside, compared to the temperature outside, it felt almost cosy, especially near the stove. He began to feel better, and bolstered by warm drinks and some bread, and he answered the many questions his new fellow prisoners asked as best he could.

Altogether, they had marched almost one hundred and forty miles in ten days, in temperatures that rarely rose above minus five centigrade and often dropped below minus twenty. As Sam fell into an exhausted sleep, he realised how his inner mental strength had got him through despite the state of his struggling physical weakness. The power of mind over matter surprised him and encouraged him at the same time. He knew that given some time for his wounds to heal, he would be ready to face whatever challenges this bloody and unpredictable war could throw at him.

He just grimly hoped that he wouldn't need to be tested any further.

Chapter 8.   WLA In Wales 1943-4

Many land girls lived in the farms where they worked. However, in many rural areas, living conditions could be very basic and the lifestyle lonely. As larger numbers of women were recruited, hostels were set up to house land girls. By 1944, there were 22,000 land girls living in 700 hostels.

There were up to 400,000 German POW's in the UK. As a rule, those whose surnames began with a letter in the first half of the alphabet were sent to the United States of America. Those whose names began with a letter in the second half of the alphabet were transported to the United Kingdom. Because of labour shortages at the end of the war, about 30,000 of them were invited to and decided to stay in the UK after the war.

Christine found the land army set up in St Mellons, near Cardiff, where she was sent to be with her sister, very different from what she had been used to in Suffolk. For a start, she was now based in a hostel, sharing with ten other girls. She had warm water to wash in and meals provided for them by their hostel's 'Mother', Annie Jones. The other girls were very friendly, and although many had their own sad war tales to tell, they were very sympathetic to Christine and looked after her.

She now worked at a number of farms in the land between Cardiff and Newport, not just one farmer. She undertook a much wider range of activities than she had working for Farmer James, and these were much more interesting. From helping with the dairy herd, milking, and looking after the doe-eyed calves to picking fruit, especially blackcurrants.

At the hostel, Elsie and Christine had top bunks next to each other. There were two bathrooms between all twenty girls, which meant queues for the baths when we all wanted to get ready to go out. Christine didn't use the showers at first because she wasn't used to them and had never really tried them before. They were a row made of galvanised steel and divided into cubicles. Christine started to use them one day when she became tired of waiting for a bath. As soon as she stood under the shower, she understood. The water was lovely, and she really enjoyed the experience. It felt like all her worries were being washed away as well as she stood there. She not only felt clean, but energised as a result. So, as though she loved a soak in the bath she chose to shower more and more often.

The village was a mile away from the hostel. Arm in arm the girls would often walk home from local dances singing songs. They wore woolly socks and small shoes and, on the way home, often took them off and walked in stockings. The villagers sometimes complained about the noise from the singing so they were told to quieten down.

One night, Christine woke up to the sound of someone whistling. It didn't sound like a bird and was different, not like anything she'd ever heard before. No one else was awake. The next day, she asked the girls if they had heard the noise and none of them had. They asked her if it was an owl or if she thought I'd been dreaming, but she hadn't. The next night, it woke her again; it whistled and sang for a long time and then stopped, only to start again soon after.

The next day, she asked the warden, and everyone tried to make suggestions, like a squeaky gate. Christine and the other girls began to dig up the land around the hostel to grow their own vegetables. While working there one day, Christine saw the postboy and called him over. "What was that sound," she asked him because she knew he might know what the sound was as he lived nearby. " I 've never heard a sound like it."

You're very blessed, "You've heard the nightingale! It comes every year about this time to the copse by the hostel and stays only for a few nights. It's supposed to bring good luck to anyone theat hears it," he smiled

 She immediately thought of Sam and wanted so much to tell him. He had been so good at recognising bird songs.

One evening a senior grey-haired lady from the WLA visited the hostel and then addressed them after dinner.

"Girls, as you know, we are still short of labour on the farms, and although we are winning the war at sea, it is vital that we produce as much food as possible" She paused, looking around slightly nervously.

"The War Office has decided to make use of German prisoners to work with us on the farms.

"You know that German POWs are imprisoned in the nearby camp in Llanmartin, just the other side of Newport. Well, they have been given the choice of volunteering to work on farms rather than languish in their camps. They will all be carefully vetted to ensure they are of no risk, and they will all have volunteered."

There was a murmuring of discontent among the girls, many of whom had lost relatives or friends in the war so far.

"What's important is that we can feed our troops and everyone at home, and if we can use them to do that, we should," she continued.

After answering a few questions, she left and the girls chatted to each other about it, but not for long, as they were tired.

Christine was nervous about first seeing them and wondered how she would feel about them. Would she feel hatred and bitterness towards the people who had killed her parents and captured Sam? She felt quite disturbed and anxious about it, but she decided she would have as little to do with them as she could and thus avoid the problem altogether for now.

It had been so long since she had seen or even heard from Sam. She hoped he was ok but she really had no idea. She wondered how much he had changed. His experiences were bound to have affected him. She had loved his charm and easy good humour, characteristics that would be sorely tested, she guessed, in a POW camp. She had changed so much, too. Late teens were always a mixed time for anyone growing up, and she had faced her fair share of challenges in the last few years as well. She had developed a resilience to get her through things but also a nervousness of what might happen. She was still relatively shy, though she had inherent warmth, inquisitiveness and a gentle sense of humour that always helped her to get on easily with others. What she still longed for was a quieter, more settled life and to bring up a family. Would Sam still be the man for her, it was becoming a bigger question as time passed by.

One lunchtime, as she sat eating her sandwiches sitting in the field she noticed and started watching a colony of ants at work. They were marching along between the clumps of grass. The sun was shining, and a cool breeze was blowing. They were going about their work in a machine-like way. It brought back memories of more happy and settled times as she remembered she had watched the ants like this when she was a little girl in her garden in London. It was fascinating to look into their complicated and alien world.

So much had passed by since then: her evacuation to Luton, the blitz, living in Shropshire, meeting Sam, joining the Land Army, losing her parents, and she had forgotten all about ants. Life felt so different now. Christine felt so different now. The ants, though, were there, always doing the same things, always marching, and they still looked exactly the same. They were always there in the background, working away. It suddenly struck her that she could find some comfort in this background. This silent fabric of life that was always there and always would be.

Her sister Elsie was her rock, and they had always been close. Now they were even closer, having gone through the loss of their parents and now being able to see each other every day. Elsie worked at a farm called 'Bluebell Farm, about halfway between Cardiff and Newport. She had worked there since joining up and was skilled in a wide range of farm duties, from milking to driving tractors to even helping with calving. The Jones farming family were very kind to her and found her invaluable. Their son Fred, in particular, was especially fond of Elsie, and she noticed that these feelings were being reciprocated more and more by her sister. Christine was very happy for her, though a little jealous. She had met Fred, a quiet man, and liked him instantly as he did her.

One morning, she cycled to work as normal. It was about a five-mile ride, and in good weather, she loved it. The roads were empty and although the route was a little hilly, she was fit from the outdoor life. She loved the smells of the changing seasons as different crops came ready for harvest. Today was the start of the fruit harvest, in particular, blackcurrants. She didn't really enjoy this as much as other farm activities as it was back-aching work, but the day was warm and sunny, and she breathed in the air of new life. It was such an escape from the misery of wartime.

She arrived at the farm and although she knew that the arrival of German POWs was imminent, it still took her by surprise to see three of them there when she arrived. Two of them were in their twenties and seemed typical of the description the Germans had promoted about the master race. They were blonde and blue-eyed and had a serious look about them. The third man was older, in his forties, she guessed. He was about five foot nine, black hair and slightly balding. He had a pleasant smile and look about him, it seemed, and Christine hoped that if she was to be working with any of them, then it would be him

They had been told in their briefing not to fraternise with the prisoners, and Christine had every intention of carrying this out. The two younger men were chatting to each other and grinning which immediately raised her defences.

They worked hard all morning and the only opportunity to talk was when they came to empty their picking baskets into the main carrier. She tried to make sure that when she did this she would be the only one, and she had succeeded in this plan so far. Soon, it was lunch break, and Christine sat on her own, enjoying the warm sunshine and eating the sandwiches that Annie from the hostel had prepared for her. Annie was a real gem. She was in her late forties and looked after Christine and the others as if she were her Mum. Christine was her favourite, though. Everyone called her Aunt Annie.

As she sat there in the sun, she looked across at the German prisoners. The two younger ones seemed to be talking and laughing together, occasionally looking her way. She felt they were talking about her, and she again felt irritated by them. The older German seemed to notice this and walked over. To her surprise, he spoke to her in almost perfect English.

"Good afternoon. I am sorry to interrupt your lunch, but I could see you were beginning to get annoyed by those two, and I wanted to explain. My name is Kurt Miller," and then he bowed slightly.

"Good afternoon to you" replied Christine shyly. "It's ok," she added.

"If I might explain. They are young men, and this is their first day out of the camp. Everything is new and free for them. They are happy that their war is over, and maybe soon they can go home."

"That's ok. I didn't mind, really," replied Christine with a white lie.

"May I talk some more? I would like to know what news you have of the war. My family is in the east of Germany, and I am very worried about them."

"We are not really supposed to talk with you," said Christine, although she could see he was being very polite, and she really felt sorry for him and his family. "But I suppose a little would be fine," she smiled, and he smiled back in relief.

"I am a teacher in English in a school in Leipzig. I did not want to fight in this war, but I had no choice. None of us did. I have a wife and a lovely young daughter, and I am so worried about them. I have not heard from them for six months."

Christine told him all the news she knew, not that it was very comforting to him as it confirmed his worries about the Russians being likely to take Leipzig ahead of the Allies. He hoped his family would be all right as he had made plans on his last visit home for them to flee to Hanover to stay with friends if it looked like the Russians would get to Leipzig first.

She asked him many questions about Germany and the war. She wanted to know if everyone liked Hitler, as she was led to believe in Britain. He replied honestly that, of course, there were some, and also others had been indoctrinated. Some followed him out of despair at the conditions between wars. He believed that the vast majority wanted a peaceful life. Germany, he said, was the land and birthplace of liberal philosophy, not cruel fanaticism, and he had been proud of this legacy until the rise of Hitler.

Over the following weeks, they developed a friendship of sorts, and Christine told him all about Sam and his imprisonment and how worried she was about him. She came to understand, through her conversations with him how it was stupid, mad people who started wars, and all most ordinary decent people like Kurt and herself wanted peaceful lives and to get on with one another.

And so, summer dissolved into autumn, and soon winter arrived. It was a quieter time of year on the farm, and somehow, like the ants, she worked her way routinely through it. Soon, it was spring, and along with it came the hope that the end of the year could possibly be in sight. With that came the renewed hope that she might see Sam again. She knew, though, that the chaos that accompanied the end of the war could also be very dangerous for him.

As April drifted into May, Christine could hear from the daily BBC news bulletin that the end of the war was near. Each night, she,

Elsie and her friends, which is now what they all were at the hostel, gathered around the radio to listen to the latest news. Each time they had listened in the last few weeks, they had expected to hear it was all over. There had been rumours that Hitler had killed himself on 1st May, and this was soon confirmed. On May 7, 1945, a sense of anticipation was hanging in the air. People across Wales and far beyond knew the Second World War was coming to an end soon.

It was now just a matter of waiting.

Did this mean it was all over? By the 6th of May, they knew it was and that Churchill would be making an announcement the next day. Celebrations were being planned everywhere.

All the girls at the hostel had the day off and decided to cycle into Cardiff for the celebrations. On every road, they passed chairs that were out in the streets, ready for street parties. In one street, they spanned nearly half the length of the street, and a stage had even been erected in the middle. There was music playing and people singing, simply glad to be alive. Yet some of the houses had their curtains drawn with the residents shut inside. Where these people had come out to watch she noticed they would often be crying rather than laughing and smiling. Christine stopped and asked a lady in one street about this, "Why have some houses closed their curtains? Do you know?"

"Those families have lost the man of the house, lovely, or one of the grown-up children serving in the forces." She replied sadly.

Christine knew how they felt. She would never get over the loss of her wonderful parents. They had given her and Elsie so much in their lives. To see them lose their lives in such an arbitrary and

133

unnecessary way had been heartbreaking - how they would have loved these celebrations. She wondered if Sam was alive, or if so what he was doing and where he was at that moment. Why hadn't they met when there was no war? But, of course, she thought, without the war, they would never have met anyway.

They arrived in the centre of Cardiff by lunchtime, and the city streets were packed with people milling around. Christine must have been hugged and kissed twenty times in the first hour by men and women who she didn't even know.

By mid-afternoon, everyone was gathered in groups around their radios as an announcement from Winston Churchill was to be made at three pm. The suspense was hard to bear. Then suddenly, there it was. The BBC announcer, in his frightfully posh accent, said the words they had all waited for so long.

"The Prime Minister, The Right Honourable Mr Winston Churchill has an announcement to make."

The unmistakable sound of Churchill's emotive voice came on the radio. His speeches, with their use of language, metaphor and powerful imagery, delivering with such authority, had strengthened the nation's resolve during the darkest of days. Christine loved to hear him talk, and the anticipation of what they all hoped he was about to say was unbearable

"Yesterday morning at 2:41 a.m. at Headquarters, General Jodl, the representative of the German High Command, and Grand Admiral Doenitz, the designated head of the German State, signed the act of unconditional surrender of all German Land, sea, and air forces in Europe to the Allied Expeditionary Force, and simultaneously to the Soviet High Command."

This was followed by more words from Churchill, by the words of a BBC correspondent.

"In the small hours of this morning, May 7th, 1945, I saw the formal acknowledgement by Germany's present leaders of their country's complete and utter defeat by land, in the air and at sea. The whole ceremony was carried out on a cold and business-like basis. If the sense of drama was there, and it was, it was because we carried it in our own hearts, remembering that this meant liberation, freedom from suffering and spared lives for countless thousands in tortured Europe."

Everyone burst into a loud cheer and just jumped around wildly, and Christine received another round of enthusiastic hugs from friends and strangers alike. The celebration lasted for hours and it was so good to see so many people so happy and relieved.

In the evening, Christine, Elsie and her WLA friends went to a buffet and danced in the ballroom above the Regal Cinema. The buffet was meagre but that didn't matter, as their appetites were satisfied by just the end of hostilities.

That night, all the street lights that were still working came on for the first time in nearly five years, and to cycle home and see the lights on in every house blazing out was magic after those long, dark years of war. Some of the shops had their windows ablaze with light.

Life was going to get better from now on, wasn't it? She thought, or at least hoped.

Chapter 9.   Liberation & Escape 1944

Allied prisoners liberated by the Russians were used as a bargaining tool in negotiations with the British about their return in exchange for Polish prisoners. They were kept up to a month, and some were never to be released, being taken to Odessa, supposedly en route to home and probably ending their lives in Russian Gulags.

During the war, the Germans captured over five and a half million Russian prisoners. Of these, three point seven million died in POW camps. Despite the fact that Stalin's own son had been taken prisoner, the Kremlin's official view was that all Russians who had 'allowed' themselves to be taken prisoner were traitors and should be shot. Many of those who had somehow survived the inhumanities of their years in prison camps were never to enjoy liberation, either being shot or put into forced labour.

There was an eerie calm about the camp throughout that Sunday, the 22nd of April 1945. The news from the BBC had revealed little about the situation in their area. The stream of refugees walking past the camp had increased daily from an initial trickle to now a flood. Many of these were skeletal, and the procession looked like something from a horror story. Rumours began to circulate around the camp about horrific death camps that were being used to eradicate Jews and that these stumbling semi-corpses in their striped clothing were the remnants from these camps that had somehow been relieved or abandoned.

New prisoners also poured into the camp. Many of these had been incarcerated for a long time but had been moved into the camp, like Sam, a month earlier, as their original camps came under threat by the Russians or Allies. The camp was full to the brim and overflowing. Men were forced to share beds, sleeping head to toe.

Very few left the hut that day. The sound of gunfire in the east seemed to be making the guards very edgy and nervous. No one wanted to tempt the goons into a rash response when they appeared to be so close to liberation. Even at roll call, they had resisted the temptation to tease the hated guard 'Blondie,' who was trying to be as creatively sadistic as possible, using any excuse to hit a man with his rifle butt. As a result, it was completed in record time.

All day Sam listened to the noise of battle, as it seemed to edge closer. Occasionally, he would gaze out of the window and see smoke and sometimes flashes of gunfire, too. He allowed himself to imagine freedom and how he would surprise Christine by visiting her at her parent's house in London when he got back. He remembered the two visits he had made to Christine there after she had returned from Shropshire and while he was undergoing his training in Northern Ireland. It had been his first time in the capital city, and even in its bomb-damaged condition, he was amazed at the splendour of the buildings and parks. He was determined to make this his first port of call when he got back.

It was almost dark when the meagre potato ration was delivered to the hut, and Sam, like most of the others, was dozing when it did. Although 'spuds' were pretty unappetising, they were filling, and during the last few weeks, almost all they were given. Sam got to work with others washing and cooking them and then serving up the steaming starch mess to the others. There was only a little nervous, slightly forced conversation. The sound of big guns was definitely becoming louder, though, and they could even hear the occasional rifle fire. Sam had been through too much to let his hopes rise too high yet. Knowing that captivity was coming to an end certainly was a peculiar feeling, but he still did not know what kind of end it was to be. As it turned out he was right to be cautious.

After consuming their starchy, tasteless meal, Sam returned to his bunk, as did everyone else. There was nothing else they could do. He slept little that night. Apart from the discomfort of sharing a bunk, a stream of confusing thoughts went through his mind. Some were comforting and even exciting, but many were frightening. He shared a few whispered thoughts with his new bunkmate Neil, another midlands lad about the same age as him.

Eventually, he must have dozed fitfully off as the next thing he was conscious of was being awakened abruptly, with everybody else, by a loud shouting outside. "The Goon Box is empty! They've all bloody gone!" They all dashed to the window to see for themselves. It was true; it was all over, wasn't it?

During the night, it appeared the guards had exercised discretion in the face of the advancing Red Army and departed with good reason heading towards the Yank lines, preferring capture by them to a very probable grizzly end if they waited for the Russians to arrive. A mighty roar spread from compound to compound. It was the resounding sound of freedom at long last.

Sam rushed outside. Even the rank air felt like it had a tinge of freedom in it. The gates were wide open, and in the distance, he could see what looked like Russian cavalry riding towards them.

"They are Cossacks," someone shouted.

The distinctive woollen hats and long swords of the Cossacks were iconic military figures.

Amazingly, the normally grey, sombre camp was already being festooned with the colourful flags of all nations that had obviously been carefully hidden away until now. Along with celebrations, this also resulted in some skirmishes between inmates. Many in the camp, like Sam, had been captured in Italy before they surrendered. The Italians, in their haste or nationalist pride, had somehow raised their flag above the Union Jack and caused anger amongst the Brits especially. Some fighting broke out, but as the Brits outnumbered the Italians, the flag order was soon changed without any serious injuries.

Soon, the Cossack cavalry arrived at the camp, and as they drew closer, Sam was amazed to realise many of them were women! A group of four of them rode through the camp and released the Russian sector. The Goons had wisely left them locked in, fearing reprisals before they could get far enough away. Sam watched as a female Cossack rider galloped around the huts. She was coarse featured and not pretty even to men who had seen few women for such a long time. She had a rifle slung over her back, a pistol stuffed in her belt, wore crossed bandoliers of ammunition and wielded a dangerous-looking sabre. She was nailing notices up in badly worded English warning all prisoners not wearing Russian uniforms to stay in their huts, or they would be shot. Sam and the others did not need any further warning and retired, temporarily at least, to their huts until the initial excitement died down. He wondered what to do next as he and the others looked out through the windows.

Many of the released Russian prisoners were being marched out of the gates, hopefully, thought Sam and the others, to be hospitalised and looked after. Although they had been in the same camp together, they had been treated in a totally different way by the Germans. They had been given little food and given the worse jobs like cleaning the latrines. Blondie, the worst goon, tormented them incessantly and shot any of them who showed the least sign of dissent. The other prisoners helped them if they could, sneaking food and cigarettes to them when they could, though they would have been punished if they were caught, especially by the cruel, vindictive Blondie.

The smell of decaying bodies from that sector had been sickening. Over the last few weeks, the Russians never reported that anyone had died in order to keep drawing that soldier's meagre rations. As a result, decaying bodies were still tied up outside the huts. The goons had not ventured close enough to find out if they were alive or not. A few days previously, the Germans, becoming ever fewer in numbers, stopped sending guards in and decided to use fierce dogs instead. They sent them in one evening with the sounds of barking and howling. Curiously, this noise quickly died down, and with just a few yelps all went quiet. In the morning, there were no dogs to be seen again, just, to the grim amusement of Sam and the other POWs, a few dog-shaped pelts hanging up on the fence.

After a while, things were quieter outside. Sam looked outside again and saw that the remaining Russian POWs were setting fire to their huts. Many men had now left their huts and were crowded around, looking into the Russian compound.

"Something's up!"

He shouted to the others in the hut and then rushed outside to see what was happening. He soon wished he had not.

Some of the freed Russian POWs had been raiding the small allotment garden to find anything edible, and it was there that they found the sadistic German guard, Blondie, hiding in one of the tool sheds. He was apparently, they later learned, asleep and in a drunken stupor. Struggling and screaming, he was being dragged and steered towards a lamppost by three Russians. The female Cossack on the horse just watched on silently but did not interfere. A very skinny Russian POW had a rope, which he first slung over the lamppost and then tied one end around Blondie's feet.

Sam, along with the others, looked on at this grizzly but compelling scene. Everyone hated Blondie and had dreamed of revenge when the time came. Now, the time had come; the reality was sickening. A couple of Russians roughly knocked him off his feet while four others pulled on the other end of the rope and lifted him off the ground feet first. Blondie was vainly grabbing at tufts of grass to somehow avoid being hauled upwards. Soon, he was dangling a couple of feet off the ground and struggled for a while to try and reach up and untie himself. Soon worn out from his efforts, he hung just there moaning and babbling.

For the Russians, this torture was just beginning, but Sam could watch no more and made his way back into the hut. He couldn't bear what was likely to happen next. He had seen enough of brutality, killings and sadism. He just wanted to get home. He returned to his bunk, took out the photo of Christine and withdrew into his fantasy world of living in peace with her after the war. He slowly returned to the hut and closed the door to try and blank out the noise outside.

After a few hours, a number of Cossack officers arrived. They knocked on the huts and indicated they would like the men to assemble outside. Sam joined the others with a mixture of excitement and apprehension. It was hard not to look across at the mutilated, bloodied and now half-naked corpse of Blondie, now missing hands and feet and still hanging upside down from the post,

The men now gathered around an obviously senior Russian officer looking at his smart uniform with red epaulettes, numerous medals and an enormous and bountiful moustache. He spoke via an interpreter who relayed his words in faulty English but clear enough for him to be understood.

"You have been rescued by the brave soldiers of the 5th Don Cossack Calvary Regiment of the magnificent Red Army. You stay near the camp for your own safety until we arrange your release to armies of the west. You are free to roam outside the camp for supplies, and we will let you know more information when we can."

The POWs let out an enormous cheer, and he smiled, waved and saluted before riding off.

Now, the British sector commander, Captain Archer, moved forward.

"Men, this is the day we have all waited for. It is still dangerous out there, and having survived for this long, we don't want to lose any other men because of stupid accidents. Your NCOs will organise you into teams to scout around for food, but let's not roam more than five miles from camp, eh. We have a few weapons left by the Goons, and each group must make sure they have at least one if they leave camp. If only we had some beer to celebrate, eh!" with that, he moved off with his NCOs to discuss how to organise details, Sam guessed.

It felt strange after so long living a half-life at the beck and call of the Goons. Now they had to think for themselves, and it was quite an adjustment. Sam and his muckers walked out of the gates just because they could, though any minute, they expected the alarm being raised and shots being fired. Outside the camp, it looked like the whole world was on the move, walking west. He could understand the CO's concerns when he looked around. They wandered back to the hut and conditioned as they were, waited for orders of what to do next.

Sgt Brian Elder arrived in their hut a few hours later. He was looking for volunteers to go out of the camp and look for food and arms. He had been impressed with the way Sam had taken responsibility for duties over the past weeks and noticed how other men had started to look at him. He turned his gaze to Sam, who immediately nodded.

"Sam, you can lead one party. You have spent more time outside camp than most, so you know how to look after yourself. Try not to wander too far and keep away from trouble. Pick up any news you can about what's going on out there."

Sam was joined by his two muckers, Robbie and Frank and his bunkmate, Neil. They got their gear together and took the only weapon available, a German Luger pistol. Normally, this would have been stowed away by one of the prisoners as a prize, but given the circumstances, it had been reluctantly donated for the purpose by one of the men in the hut who had found it, with a "Don't you bloody lose this. I want it back."

Sam smiled and he had learned that captured Lugers were much prized by Allied soldiers during the war as trophies. However, German soldiers were aware of this and would use Lugers as 'bait', rigging them to detonate land mines or hidden booby traps when disturbed. This tactic had become common enough to make more experienced Allied soldiers deeply suspicious of any apparently discarded Luger that they discovered.

They left the camp cautiously, still with that strange feeling that they might be ordered to stop after their time of captivity. As they made their way towards the nearest village, they passed some horrific sights. Obviously not all of the guards had made it to safety. He could see several of them hanging from trees, crows already getting to work on them. Not just guards either, as they came across a whole German family comprising of what looked like husband and wife, and three young children aged between eight and thirteen. Sam and several of the group retched in horror, and they moved on quickly.

The countryside that had been a mass of noise and movement only days ago was now eerily quiet and still. The quiet was occasionally pierced by the sound of shots and shells and, sometimes, occasional screams. Soon, the nearest village came into view. It appeared to be undamaged, with no fires burning. Nobody was to be seen, and they started knocking on doors, but with no response.

"There's someone in this one I can see," shouted Neil, "but he's pretending not to see me."

"Well, we need supplies and they will have to share. If they won't let us in, then we'll have to break in," said Sam reluctantly.

Sam banged at the door with a brick he had found, and eventually, the lock gave. An awful spectacle awaited them when they walked inside. The family of four were all sitting around the table with their heads slumped on the table. They had all been shot in the head, apparently by the father, who was still holding a pistol after apparently shooting the others first. He realised, with horror, the scale of the fear the family had must have felt. With no time to escape and knowing what would happen to his family, they had come to this grisly conclusion. They all rushed out of the house, no longer interested in searching for anything there.

In some of the abandoned houses, they found some stores of food, such as potatoes and bread, which they collected. It was starting to get dark, and they were in dangerous territory.

"We'd better head back, lads. I'd hate to be caught out here after dark," shouted Sam. After gathering up what they had found, they started to make their way back to the camp. It was not in any way a pleasant sightseeing the results of what the Russian conquerors had been doing, raping and pillaging the land. It reminded Sam of books he had read when he was young about the barbaric raids of Attila the Hun and Genghis Khan. As they made their way to the camp, they came across many examples of hangings and bodies of civilians and troops alike, some left often after being obviously badly abused.

About a mile out from the camp, they came across an abandoned German truck. They searched it and found four revolvers and ammunition to go with them. They then walked back soberly to the camp.

They didn't talk much that night. Their emotions in turmoil. Happy to be free, horrified and sick at what they had seen. Sam didn't sleep much that night, no matter how hard he tried to concentrate on positive things like going home and seeing Christine and his family. He knew his family would be delighted to see him safe and sound, but what about Christine? She would be happy that he was safe, he was sure, but with their experiences, would they be the same? Would it be the same between them?

They made several sorties over the next few days and although they sometimes found some food, it was proving more and more dangerous and depressing. The camp CO said that they should cease for now. In fact, although the Russians were providing no information on when they were to be shipped out, they were providing adequate basic rations.

One day, another force of regular Russian troops arrived together with a tank. They searched the camp, looking for anything they could find, and several returned excitedly holding a camera. They indicated to Sam, who was looking at the tank, that they wanted him to take photos of them. He took several including one with him in it. The Russians then indicated they wanted to see the photos and got increasingly angry with Sam as he tried to explain that the film needed to be developed. They obviously knew little of how cameras worked and had been recruited from peasant stock, it appeared.

Sam eventually convinced them that they could maybe have their pictures if they took him to the chemist in the nearest small town, where he hoped they had the means to develop the film. They asked him to jump into the tank, and nervously and reluctantly, he did so. They drove the tank into the town and almost surreally 'parked' outside the pharmacy. If Sam hadn't been so nervous, he would have found it quite comical. On entering the shop, Sam explained to the pharmacist that he wanted the film developed while they were there.

The chemist shook his head and said, "nicht possible."

At this, the Russian soldiers pointed their rifles at him, and this seemed to terrify him and change his mind quite quickly. He indicated he would take ten minutes and disappeared into a back room, obviously the dark room. A Russian soldier guarded outside. Sure enough, after about ten minutes, the chemist reappeared with the photos, and the soldiers were delighted, laughing and snatching the photos off each other to look at them. They then all got back in and onto the tank and returned to the camp, leaving a very relieved pharmacist and local populace behind.

After about a week, the British sector CO called the men together and announced that the Russians had said they would allow a limited number of men to leave for Gdansk on the Baltic coast in Poland to be transported home from there.

"The Russians have said it was unsafe because of the fighting to go directly west. This will allow some of you to get home faster because, as you realise, our discussions with them about the repatriation seem to be going very slowly. I must admit I am beginning to get suspicious of them and their motives, and I find it difficult to recommend whether it's safer to stay or take this option."

Sam was definitely noticing a change of mood from the Russians. They had started out friendly and helpful. Now, they were acting more aggressively when they wanted things done. Whenever they were asked when they could leave, the answer was never straightforward, ranging from 'soon' to 'it's complicated' to 'don't worry.' It was beginning to feel more live occupation than liberation. About half the men decided to take the Gdansk option. Sam was firmly in the 'stay' camp. This was not because he thought that was a safer option but because he, together with a group of about six others, had decided to escape and make their own way to the Allied lines.

The following day, they stocked up their haversacks with bread and odd scraps salvaged from the kitchen. By now, the Russians' attitude left no doubt that should they be found moving off, they might be forcibly detained. The others readily agreed, therefore, to Sam's proposal that they should leave that night. They carefully smuggled out their packed haversacks during the day and hid them in a clump of bushes about a hundred yards down the road.

After dark, they sauntered out of the building and strolled casually down the grass verge of the roadside. Behind the bushes, they collected their haversacks and struck out across the fields. There was a bright moon, and its light was enough to show them the way. Sam had a rough idea of the direction to take from a map he had gradually developed as a result of their scouting raids during the days before. Until they were well clear of the camp, they decided to keep clear of the roads. Sam had worked out that they could circle around the outside of the main town of Muhlberg and that the river Elbe lay on the other side. Then, following the course of the Elbe until they came to a bridge, they would cross over and place themselves in the hands of the first friendly troops they came across.

By early dawn, they had covered about fifteen to twenty miles uneventfully, and the town of Muhlberg was now well behind them. It was getting lighter, and they needed to find a place to rest and sleep. An old farm building in the distance seemed to be the most suitable place. There was only an old farmer in occupation when they arrived. Although initially suspicious, after Sam convinced him of who they were, he seemed relieved and very glad of their company.

His opinion of the Russians was expressed as "Ruskie nix gut".

Most of the German population had fled across the Elbe from the advancing Russians, who, so the farmer said, had looted everything of value during their advance.

"Ruskie alzo dumkopf," he added with a twinkle in his eye and indicated he had food stored away he was willing to share with them.

Their German host then even prepared them a hot stew. Afterwards they then slept off the weariness of the night's journey in the soft hay in the barn. Shortly after mid-day, they awoke, and Sam suggested that they push on ahead for the Allied lines as quickly as they could. The farmer prepared them a cup of what passed by that time for coffee and they gratefully thanked him for all his help and wished him all the best. It was easy, Sam reflected, to hate all Germans, but during the last few years, many of them he had come into contact with were friendly, and some, like this farmer, had gone above and beyond to help. The stupidity of war, he thought again. It is governments that fight, not the majority of people.

On the road, they soon caught up with a frightened German woman who was pushing a small wooden trolley with what looked like all her worldly possessions piled on top. She was in her mid-thirties, and she relaxed as she recognised them as British.

"Please, can I go with you and take me to Americans, yes?" She begged Sam and the others.

"I am scared of the Russians and what they might do to me if they capture me. I've seen and heard about so many terrible and frightening things."

They could see she was terrified of being caught by the Russians. They huddled together to discuss the situation for a minute. Although they had worries about the complications this might cause, they all agreed, and as she spoke a certain amount of English, they felt that her help as an interpreter would also be useful.

"What's your name?" asked Sam.

"My name is Anke. I have been travelling for a few days, keeping out of sight of the Russians."

"Well, come with us," said Sam. "We'll do our best to get you to safety."

"Oh, thank you, thank you."

She said tearfully and went up to each of them and gave them all a grateful hug. They piled their haversacks onto the trolley, and taking turns to push the cart, they continued their journey.

The road seemed endless. A few trucks passed us but nobody stopped to enquire who they were. Their journey took them through one or two villages, but these had been reduced to ghost towns. All the occupied houses had large red flags hanging down from the windows to comply with Russian orders. Very few Germans remained on the streets. Occasional movements behind drawn curtains told them that frightened people were trying to catch a glimpse of their future fate. As night approached, Anke said she knew some people in the next small town, and they might be able to spend the night in their house.

The lack of restful sleep was now fast catching up with them. Sam realised how important it was for all of them to get a good night's sleep. They found the house and the large red flag, which adorned it, proved that the family had remained there. The occupant, a doctor, made them welcome. He introduced himself as Dr. Mikel Hansdorf. He showed them into what had been his consulting room and provided them with wood for a fire. A little while later, he re-entered the room with a large dish of some kind of stew, which they devoured with absolute relish. They had not tasted something so good for a very long time. Amazingly, he then brought them bread and cheese to finish off. It was glorious to enjoy the feeling of having full stomachs.

Dr Hansdorf told them of the Russian advance and of the raping and looting that had taken place. They all commiserated, but even then, it seemed very strange to Sam that he was now siding with a former enemy against a supposed current wartime ally.

The following day, they moved off towards the Elbe. Anke told them there was a bridge across the river two miles away. She herself had decided to remain with the good doctor. They wished her and Mikel good luck and thanked them profusely for their help. As they left, Sam really hoped that these former enemies survived without any more drama.

They had been walking for about an hour when they came to a crossroads. Down one road came a chauffeur driven open-topped car in which sat a couple of seemingly high-ranking German officers. By this time, Sam and the rest were all armed from items they had found, usually on dead bodies along the way. Sam pointed his gun at them along with the others and stopped them.

"Where are you going?" said Sam.

"To the American lines, so get out of our way. We have important things to discuss with them."

They replied officiously in a way that reminded the men of some of the arrogant officers they had experienced at the camps.

"You're going the wrong way," Sam said after a little thought about their attitude. "You should go this way."

He pointed to where Sam and his team had just come from. One of Sam's mates had to look away so as not to give the game away by his wide grin when he realised what Sam was up to.

"I'm afraid you will have to get out and walk out. You won't need your car."

The Germans started arguing dismissively, but as soon as Sam and the others pointed their revolvers, they instantly became more receptive. They took everything they had except the car. It didn't seem a wise idea to drive a German car, though it was tempting. Sam's watch was stolen in 1943, so he took one of theirs. They grabbed binoculars and any food and then saw them on their way - towards the Russians.

After walking on for about another half an hour along the main road, they came to the bridge. As they drew closer, Sam noticed a small wooden hut at the side of the entrance and a wooden pole placed on two trestles straddled the road. A Russian flag flew overhead and an armed Russian armed sentry was standing outside the hut. Another guard was pacing the bridge to the centre; the other half of the bridge was being patrolled by what seemed to be an American soldier, possibly an officer.

They all relaxed as they realised they were going to be free at last. As they drew closer, waving their arms happily, instead of welcoming them, the Russian outside the hut stopped them and grimly pointed his gun at them. Sam tried to explain to him that they were British and that they wished to cross over the bridge. He appeared confused and disappeared inside and emerged again a minute later accompanied by an officer, who didn't look like he was going to be any more helpful.

Luckily, the US officer on the bridge, seeing their predicament, came across and conferred with the Russians. The American was very pleasant and introduced himself as Benjamin.

"But call me Ben," he smiled.

He shook hands with all of them, saying that they would soon be on their way home, but first, the Russians wanted proof of their identity before they would let them cross the bridge. This was an incredible relief as it was quite easy to provide identity as they had their paybooks and Stalag identity cards. After scrutinising them importantly for what seemed an age, the Russian officer handed them back and shouted a command to the sentry. They were suddenly allowed to cross, to freedom that had many times seemed beyond Sam's grasp. Ben hastily obtained a jeep, and they were taken to their barracks. While waiting for the jeep to arrive Sam chatted to the Americans on guard at the bridge. They all had a pretty poor opinion of their Russian allies.

As they bumped along in the jeep, *finally*, thought Sam that he was free and on his way home. He had been through so much in the last eighteen months, but no more, he reflected, than many others, and in many ways, often due to the kindness of his 'enemies.' He had been lucky. He had changed, too. His thoughts led him to wonder how the war had affected Christine and whether they would still want to be together when they met after all this time. Not if when he thought crossly. After all, he had been through, he felt he must be positive and not fall into being negative whatever the future held. And then he smiled wistfully about how life could yet be

After about thirty minutes, they arrived at the American camp. They had taken over a large castle-like building and its various outbuildings. They were taken to a large room with real beds. They were asked politely to strip and take a shower and told that they would be provided with fresh new clothes. Sam realised they must be rather rank by now, and the thought of a shower with real soap before lying in a real bed was heavenly. They showered, shaved and dressed in their new clothes. He and his mates were beginning to feel human again. Before going to the mess to eat, they were asked to go for debriefing. Sam told them all he knew, especially about the chaos in the Russian-occupied areas. The American officer, then, thinking out loud, said:

"Why are we stopping here then? Why not push the bloody Ruskies back as well? I have such a bad feeling about what's going on. We ought to sort them out too now, or we'll have to do it all over again someday, I'm sure."

From the scenes Sam had experienced, he thought this was probably right, but as for continuing the war to do this. No, he had had enough, more than enough.

Sam joined his mates in the mess and they had another great meal of chicken stew followed by fruitcake with condensed milk. His stomach could hardly believe what was going on. The American officer joined them and said they should be able to get a flight to the RAF base at Hanover tomorrow and then onward with the RAF back to England. England thought Sam, and home and Christine. For a lad who had hardly been out of Shropshire before the war, he could hardly believe he had been away for two long years. He was exhausted and made his way back to the bunk room, and there sank slowly and deeply into the first real sleep, in freedom, for almost two years.

The following morning, after breakfast, they reported to the C.O. He said, "I've got some frustrating news for you, I'm afraid. We can't fly you out for at least a week. Its chaos still out there, as you know, and we have to carry out emergency food drops. There are ordinary German people out there who are having a very rough time, and we have discovered their so-called labour camps with conditions you wouldn't believe possible."

He stopped for a moment and almost welled up as he remembered what he had seen.

"We have to help them first as I'm sure you realise."

Sam and the others nodded sadly, but he couldn't believe that, yet again, his journey home was to be delayed.

"Is there any other way to get to Hanover?" he asked urgently.

"Well, there is nothing organised. I'm sure you can cadge lifts in that direction, although it's still a little risky, but you'll get there, I'm certain, if that's what you want to do."

He looked at Sam and could see the urgency in the young man's weary eyes.

"Hang on, I think there may be a truck going to our base near Leipzig. If you can get there, I'm sure you'll manage to get on to Hanover."

Two days later, by dint of his perseverance and to his great relief, he entered the RAF base at Hanover. The country he had travelled through was in a state of turmoil. Ordinary German people were doing what they needed to do to survive, often begging and sometimes looting. Mostly they were acting out of desperation, but he could see examples of exploitation too, where some were taking advantage of the chaos.

He was welcomed into the camp and it was arranged for him to fly out the next day. He flew to England the following morning in a Lancaster Bomber flown by an Australian crew. He had never been in an aircraft before and although it was exciting it was unnerving. The crew were very friendly and gave him some blankets for warmth, saying, "It gets as cold as a well digger arse at fifteen thousand feet, matey."

The accent and colourful language made Sam smile. He wearily nodded his thanks. He had never met Australians before and wondered how many more nations had been involved in this damn war. Although very tired Sam was determined to stay awake to see the iconic white cliffs of Dover. Even given the uncomfortable surroundings, the cold, the engine noise, and his efforts, he soon succumbed to a deep sleep and only awoke again as the plane noisily came to land at Watford.

He was met by several smiling ladies from the Women's Voluntary Service, armed with char and wad (tea and cake) in one hand and syringes in the other. One of them came towards him, brandishing an ugly-looking syringe, which she tried to force down the back of his neck.

"What's that for?" Sam cried, pushing her away. "Delousing!" She replied.

He gave in to the necessary treatment. What a welcome home, thought Sam.

Chapter 10.   June 1945

At the end of the war, the government was faced with the enormous challenge of integrating thousands of troops back into society. As a result, they planned to do this gradually not releasing troops from the army completely for up to two years after the war.

They were worried about social unrest and housing, especially given the bomb damage.

After what seemed an unending two-day debriefing at Watford, Sam was eventually given a rail pass and one month's leave. His first thought after writing to his mum to say he was back in the country safely, was to try and find Christine and meet her again. He decided the best plan was to visit her parents in London where he had visited them before embarking for North Africa.

He boarded a train from Watford Junction headed for London Euston. It was packed and there was standing room only. As he travelled through the outskirts of London, he could already see some of the damage caused by the bombing and started to worry even more about what he would find.

He had gone through so much during the war and went through it in his head as the train trundled onwards. The events at Anzio, his capture and the terrible journey to Germany, his illness, the long march, the Stalags, the liberation by the Russians and its dreadful consequences, his escape and the help he had received, and the final journey back to England. All this had changed him, and he was undoubtedly a very different person from the naive country lad who had left British shores all those long months ago.

He had only scant news about Christine and received only one letter from her while he was a POW. This was, he hoped, because of the difficulty in getting mail and not because of the nagging worry that sometimes ran through his heart like the chill of an icy wind that she had lost interest in him. She must have been through a lot, too. He worryingly knew the Americans had spent time in the UK preparing for the D-Day landings, and he had heard stories about how they had been attractive to many British girls with their new music and better rations.

The train slowly hissed and shuddered its way into Euston station, and he, along with many returning fellow soldiers, disembarked. Some had relatives, wives and children waiting for them, and there were emotional scenes all around him as he made his way down to the Tube. The Underground had amazingly survived well despite the attempts of the German blitzkrieg and soon he arrived at Kentish Town, the nearest stop to Christine's parent's house.

He eagerly walked half a mile or so down the road towards their house, and as he drew closer, he could hardly recognise things. Some of the houses had been badly damaged, and he tried to make out where her house was. A sudden sense of fear ran through him like the chill of an icy wind. He slowly realised, to his horror, their house no longer existed. In its place was just a pile of rubble with kids playing around in the ruins. It took a while for the shock of the reality to register. Was Christine all right? Were her parents all right? A huge weight suddenly seemed to be crushing his heart.

For a while, he just sat there on the remains of the garden wall, looking at the ground. He was shaking like a jelly. After all he'd been through, after all that she must have been through, he couldn't believe that it might have ended just like this. After sitting there for some time, he felt a hand on his shoulder and looked up to see a kindly lady in her fifties looking at him.

"Are you all right?" she said.

"Did you know the family that lived here?" Tell me what happened if you know anything. Please!"

"I knew them a little as I ran the shop around the corner. They weren't in the house when the bomb landed. They weren't hurt, and as far as I know, they are still ok. They went to stay with relatives somewhere else in London. Not sure where, though I'm sorry I can't be any more help."

"Are you sure they are ok? Were any family members with them at the time?" Sam asked while holding his breath and waiting for the answer.

"No, I'm quite sure. Both their daughters are away working in the land army. I hope you find who you are looking for. There has been so much sadness and disruption."

Sam felt a surge of relief flow through him and the lead weight lifting from his heart. "Thank you so much; that's the news I wanted to hear, for now at least."

With that, she smiled and walked off, leaving Sam to consider what to do next. He had no idea where Christine's parents might be, so trying to find them in London in turmoil was unlikely to be easy. An idea formed in his head at that moment. Why not go to WLA HQ in London while he was here and find out where Christine was before returning home to Shropshire? The WLA HQ, he found out from a local London 'Bobby', was in Chesham Street SW1, so he made his way there via the Circle line. The shock at seeing the ruins of

Christine's home still resonated through him. Considering the damage London had undergone, it was not surprising that her house might have been damaged. Throughout all of his time in the POW camp, he had, though somehow, always believed they would end up together. Now that belief had been badly shaken and he started wondering again what else might have happened and whether she would still love him.

When he arrived at the WLA HQ, friendly staff sent him up to an office on the second floor, where they said he would find the information he was looking for. He entered the records office, and after some searching, an efficient young lady informed him that Christine and her sister were now in South Wales, living in a WLA hostel near Cardiff. She wrote down the details for him and said that she hoped he would find her.

Home was calling, and much as he would have liked to board a train to Cardiff, his recent experiences had made him more circumspect, and he thought it might be best to find out more about what had happened to her first. Two years apart was such a long time. He sent his mother a telegram saying he would be home the next day and stayed in the local army barracks for that night.

The next morning, he travelled to Euston and caught another packed train through to Shrewsbury. As he travelled through the towns and countryside, he saw in many places the damage caused by bombing, and this was very apparent in Coventry, especially where the ruins of the cathedral were a haunting sight. Many places were not affected by war bomb damage, though, and the countryside looked as calm and beautiful as when he left. It gave him comfort to realise that so many things hadn't changed.

He arrived at Shrewsbury, and after about an hour's wait, he caught the bus to Shifnal. He had a slight hope that someone would be there to meet him but they had no idea at what time he was due to arrive. He started his five-mile walk home along the empty country roads. He was surprisingly fit after his adventures, and even carrying his gear he enjoyed the walk. As he got nearer to home, he kept expecting to be met or maybe for some welcoming committee. None was forthcoming, and when he finally reached home, it was disappointingly empty, too. No one was in. However, he couldn't believe he had made it home after all this time and smiled to himself at all the familiar objects around him and even the smells of home. But where was everybody?

He waited for over an hour until he heard some commotion outside. The back door burst open, and there was his mum, dad, three sisters and one of his brothers. They all stood for a moment and looked at each other before his mum rushed over to him in tears and gave him a huge hug.

"How did you get here?" She said. "We have waited and waited at the end of the lane, and Jack walked nearly all the way to Newport looking for you."

"I didn't come that way. I got the bus to Shifnal and walked from there. I thought you had forgotten me!"

"All we have done is wait and wait for you to get home ever since we got your letter to say you were free and with the Americans at last. It's so wonderful to see you, son." She sobbed and hugged him again and again.

When she finished, he also got the same treatment from his brothers and sisters, and even his Dad, not known for his emotions, had a tear in his eye as he gave him a very rare hug.

They were full of questions like the continuous popping of corks. His mum served him pheasant stew while he tried to answer some of them. It was his favourite, she knew, and he loved the warm, sweet country smell of it, and the taste brought so many memories of pre-war times. They had, he felt so far, avoided any mention of Christine, so as soon as he could get a question in himself, he asked had they had any news of her. His mum said

"She's all right, but she has been through an awful lot" "What?" said Sam, "Tell me, please tell me."

"Well, she started to work for the WLA in Suffolk, and I think you must have had a letter from her there, although you might not have known where because of the censoring."

"I did, I received two letters from her while I was in Italy and one later while in POW Camp, but they didn't say too much. Go on."

"Well, her Mum and Dad survived the Blitz ok, but their house was blown up by a V1 'Doodle Bug' bomb. They were both thankfully out at the time, but you can imagine how worried Christine must have been."

"Oh god, that must have been awful," said Sam.

"Well, they then went to live at first with relatives and then some friends of theirs had some spare rooms and kindly said they could move in there. Well, they moved in on a Friday and on a Sunday while they were finishing their Sunday lunch, a V2 flying bomb

163

exploded very nearby and killed them both instantly, leaving her Aunty very badly wounded."

Sam sat there in silence, with his head in his hands, taking in the news and then said quietly through his fingers,

"Oh, my poor, poor Christine, she must have been absolutely devastated."

"After the funeral," continued his Mum, "The WLA arranged for Christine to join up with her sister Elsie in South Wales, and that's where they are now. Christine wrote to me and told me not to tell you about her parents until you arrived home. She knew you would have enough on your plate. I haven't told her that you are safe and home yet. The postal service is still poor, and I thought you should be the one to let her know anyway."

"This bloody war, Mum, thank god it's over."

"She has been through a lot of experiences, and it will have changed her, Sam," said his sister Mary. "You can't expect things between you to be the exactly same as when you left. Look at you," She said while giving him yet another hug, "You look different. There is a touch of sadness about you, but at the same time, you have grown, and I can see what a strong man you have become."

"There is so much I would like to tell you about, but I feel I just can't and won't, well not at the moment anyway. I have seen stuff I never want to see again, and nobody else should have to either, and I have been one of the very lucky ones, really. It's all of you and thoughts of Christine that have kept me going. I wouldn't have survived without you all. I know I wouldn't."

And with that, he broke into tears and sobs, and his Mum and sister just hugged him for the few minutes it took him to stop and compose himself.

"What should I do now?" said Sam, recovering his composure. "I have only got four weeks to leave before I have to report to barracks in Ripon in Yorkshire for, I don't know how long."

"Four weeks after all you've been through!" She exclaimed. "Well, write to her, Sam, now this minute. Let her know you are home and well, and just test the water. Say you would like to see her and see how she replies. You two were so good together. But don't get your hopes too high. I would hate for you to be hurt even more," said Mary.

"Thanks, Mary, that's very sensible. If you don't mind everyone, I want to do that right now, and I am very tired. But I'm so very happy to be home with you all at last."

With that, he picked up his kit back gave his mum and sisters a kiss and retired to his room to try and write something to Christine. After a lot of reflection and several failed attempts, he wrote:

My dearest Christine,

I can't fully believe it myself, but I have arrived home in Shropshire. Mum has told me all your news, and I am so so sorry to hear about your parents and your Aunty Flo. It must have been so awful for you.

As you can imagine, life has not been easy for me over the last eighteen months since I was captured. I can't believe it's been almost two years since we said goodbye.

165

I have thought of you a lot during all that time, especially when Beetlejuice was shining in the sky, hoping that one day we would see each other again. I know so much has happened to you and I'm sure you must have made many new friends, too.

I would love to come and see you down in South Wales. Tell me if you would like that too. I have only four weeks before I have to go back to the barracks

With my love, Sam. xx

After reading this over several times he hoped he had set the right tone. He wanted to get it right and show how he felt without being too pushy. Satisfied, he rushed downstairs

"What time the post, Mum? Will I catch it?"

His mum smiled and said he had an hour yet, and she gave him a stamp for the envelope. Bethan asked if she could walk down to the post box about half a mile away with him, and he was delighted to have her with him. As they walked, they talked happily together about events locally. Sam felt relaxed, excited and anxious all at the same time. They posted the letter, and he wished he had some way of speeding up the process. He even managed to dawdle around the box to make sure the postman collected the mail, and when he was sure he had done so, they walked off.

"You have it bad, big brother," said Beth, smiling. Sam gave her a playful push in reply.

The next few days were a torment for him, checking the mail every day. Four days later a letter for him arrived, and he ran out into the garden to sit on the garden seat and read it. Holding his breath, he opened it slowly and then read the contents.

My dearest Sam,

How absolutely wonderful to hear you have returned home safely. Elsie and I danced around the room in excitement and delight.

We have been through some dark times, and without my sister Elsie, I'm not sure I would have made it in any decent shape. But I am fine, honestly and enjoying life much more down here than I did in Suffolk.

What about you, though? You must tell me all you can about it. Elsie and I would love to see you. Let me know when you are coming. We can arrange to put you up on a local farm where Elsie has fallen for the Farmer's son, Fred Jones. I am still working for the WLA, though things have relaxed, and I am owed some leave.

You can get the train to Newport (yes, another one, not the one near you) and a bus from there to a place called St Mellons. From there, it's about a two-mile walk up the lane to the farm called Tan Y Waun, a bit of a mouthful, I know. They will expect you.

I will arrange for Beetlejuice to be shining. Lots of love.

Christine xx

At first reading, he was delighted she wanted to see him. On second reading, he wasn't sure whether this would be purely as a friend. The 'Elsie and I' bit concerned him a little. Why not say she alone?

Was he reading too much into this? There was only one way to find out, so he wrote a reply saying he would be down the day after next, which was a Saturday.

The train journey was quite straightforward via Birmingham, Gloucester and then Newport and after catching the bus to St Mellons, he started his walk to the farm following Christine's directions. He hadn't been able to give them an exact arrival time, as timetables at the moment seemed only to be a rough guide. As he walked along the country lanes he enjoyed the countryside, quite different to Shropshire. He suddenly noticed the sound of some skylarks and looked up. This triggered memories of that awful day in Anzio when he was captured and lost his great friend, Fergus. He must write to their family, he thought guiltily. Sadly, for a while, he walked on, almost waiting for gunfire to suddenly blast out its terror as it did that day.

The walk helped him regain his composure, and he spotted halfway down the hill in front of him, a farm, which he thought must be the one. It was a whitewashed, sturdy, two-story building, very different to the reddish stone of Shropshre. He came to the entrance where there was a whitewashed wall with the name of the farm he couldn't pronounce written neatly on a piece of grey slate. He turned into the drive, and as he walked across the yard, a man about ten years older than him with a ruddy complexion and a pleasant smile walked up to him.

"Well then, you must be Sam," he said, holding out his hand to shake hands. Great to meet you. I'm Fred. I see you found your way."

He had a gentle Welsh lilt reminding him of his bunkmate and mucker in Stalag IXB. "And you too. What a lovely day and what wonderful countryside."

"Yes, we're very lucky. Come on in and meet my parents and have a cup of tea. I'm sure you need one after your journey."

Sam followed him into the old farmhouse, and he had to duck his head as he entered the low door. Fred introduced him to his mother and she made a big fuss of him and made him sit down while she made him tea. The delicious smell of something baking filled the air. The tea arrived with some unusual flat round currant cakes, obviously the source of the wonderful aroma.

"These are wonderful," said Sam tasting one.

They had a delicious, slightly spicy taste, too.

"We call them bake stones, but outside Wales, they are often called Welsh cakes," said Mrs Jones.

Fred said that Christine was working on a nearby farm but would be back in a couple of hours. Sam said that he would enjoy walking over to meet her, and Fred wrote directions on a piece of paper. So, after pinching yet another of those delicious baked stones, he headed off. After walking through the fields following the pencil map Fred had drawn, he began to make out people working in the field about half a mile away.

As he drew closer, he made out who he thought might be Christine chatting away with what looked like a good-looking man. A pang of jealousy ran through him. She looked up and saw him and immediately started to run towards him. His heart leapt as he saw it was, in fact, Christine, and he ran to meet her, too. They stopped a few feet away from each other, slightly embarrassed by their show of enthusiasm "Oh, Sam, I can't believe it's you!" "And I can't believe I'm here!"

With that, they hugged each other for what seemed an age. They then drew back and kissed each other.

"It's been so long, and you look so different," said Christine.

"You've changed too. You look quite the young woman and not the girl I left."

"Better, I hope," she smiled.

"Yes, even better." said Sam

"You haven't lost your charm, at least," she smiled. "We have so much to talk about, to ask you about and to tell each other. I am such a different person. The war has changed me, and I'm sure it's changed you. We'll have to get to know each other all over again."

"Yes, let's pretend that we have just met. What happened before is a distant dream. What happens now and how much we like each other now is important."

Christine smiled, and they hugged and kissed all over again. The man that Christine had been talking to before came over. Sam could see, to his relief, that on closer inspection, he was in his late forties. He said politely in good English but with a German accent,

"Hello, please forgive me for interrupting this wonderful reunion. My name is Kurt Miller, and Christine has told me all about you. I am a POW as you were, and I would not have come to speak, but my family is in Germany, and I am so worried about them. Have you any news you could tell me?"

Sam shook his hand.

"Of course, I would not be alive today without the brave actions of the German doctor. Where were your family living when you last heard, do you know?" They were in Leipzig, but we had made arrangements for them to go to Hanover if the Russian advance got too close to them

"I have to be honest. Everywhere the Russians had occupied was in a bad way. If your family reached Hannover, though, they would be in the American sector and would be ok now. Hannover was very badly bombed; I flew from near there on my return. There is food and medicine there now, at least, and if they made it, then things will be all right for them."

"Thank you," said Kurt. "I am sure they got there," he said unconvincingly

"Keep positive. They are registering everyone and you will soon find out. I got through, and they will have, too."

Christine gave Kurt a hug and said she would see him sometime the following week. He thanked them and walked sadly away.

"Thanks for saying that to him, Sam," she said. "He is a nice man and has become a friend. He has told me a lot of what went on in Germany."

She was delighted to realise that Sam had not developed any bitterness or resentment in his character after the treatment he had gone through.

Sam, as if reading her thoughts, said, "It's the war that's the enemy, not the people in it. It forces the best and the worst from people, and I have certainly experienced both."

"Yes, I agree so much. Holding grudges and hatred will also ruin our future lives. We must both try not to, too. Everything that has happened has just been so awful and so sad."

They looked at each other and smiled again. Sam could see how much Christine had changed. She had a gentle confidence and self-assuredness that he couldn't remember before. She was still the happy, slightly absent-minded girl as before, and the last few years had made her even prettier, he thought.

Christine thought that Sam had changed a lot. He was more serious and had certainly aged and even had some grey hairs, which was unusual for someone his age but perhaps not so when she considered what he had gone through. Underneath all that, though, the same Sam was there and could be coaxed out, she thought given time away from the war.

"I want to hear everything that's happened to you," said Christine, "or all that you feel you can," she added, noticing a slight shadow pass over his gaze as she spoke.

"And I want to hear all about you too. I was so, so sad to hear about your parents. They were so lovely to me, and I know how close you were to them."

She choked slightly as the memory flashed before her," I'll be finished here in about forty-five minutes she said, and then we can walk back together and talk. You'll love Fred and the Jones family. I think there's a good chance that Elsie and Fred are going to get engaged soon. You sit down over here and enjoy the sunshine and relax, and I'll come and get you."

Sam sat and then laid out in the sun, enjoying the warm rays of the sun on his body. He felt good. He had met Christine again after all this time. She had not forgotten him. He was surprised, though, how much his image of her was now so different from reality. She was a woman, not a girl. If anything, she was prettier than before. The naivety, though, had vanished. He would now have to build a relationship with a woman who now saw herself as an equal and not in the traditional, more subservient female role.

He was he knew different. He wanted more out of life. He felt a moral duty for his sons and daughters, if he ever had any, not to face the horrors that he had.

After a while, Christine, as promised, re-joined him, and they walked slowly back together to the Williams farm. In the hedgerow, a bird broke out into its beautiful song

"A nightingale," said Christine before Sam could say anything.

"You have become a real country girl," he smiled.

She thought to herself, yes town girl to country girl. She loved the peace and comfort of the countryside.

"And what about you? What have you become?" she teased slightly, though she was very much interested.

"I don't know. Restless at the moment, I guess. I haven't been demobbed yet. It could take up to two years, I'm told. Though they may take my time in POW camp into account, he smiled. I do want to do something with my life. I want to help stop us from getting into this mess again. But first, I need to get a job."

"I don't know what to do," said Christine. "I think I'll stay on for six months in the WLA. We're still needed. It will be a while before things get back to anything like normality. I could stay on here for a while with the Jones family as they have offered. I just want some peace and normality to hopefully bring up a family of my own. But then, who knows."

"Yes, who knows," said Sam with a wistful smile. And hand in hand, they slowly made their way back to the farm.

Chapter 11.   Cardiff 1945

In August 1946, tens of thousands of people, mainly ex-servicemen and their families, moved into empty military camps around Britain. Over the course of the occupations, more than 45,000 people were involved in the takeover of most of the military camps it achieved its greatest fame in the 'Great Sunday Squat' on 8 September, when it dominated the newsreels and newspapers for much of August and September 1946. Thousands of squatters stayed in the camps for years afterwards, but the squatters' movement disappeared from public view as quickly as it had emerged.

Same and Christine found that although they had faced many challenges and grown up and matured during this time, they were indeed a couple who had a lot going for them. They were both prepared to work hard for what they wanted, had a good sense of humour and shared the same values, and over the next five years, Sam and Christine's lives were indeed filled with peace and happiness.

They were married and after a short time living in rented accommodation, they were allocated one of the new prefab council houses in Cardiff. Their first child a girl they named Suzanne, was born in 1948, and their second, a boy named David, was born three years later. They were happy, even though rationing went on and on, and there were few luxuries.

Sam was lucky to be demobbed fairly quickly because they did indeed take his time as a POW into account. He managed to get a job as a postman very quickly and soon was promoted to run a sorting office. Although he was happy in his home life and enjoyed his job, he felt that something was missing. Had he and Christine gone through so much during the war just to now just forget about it. They both wondered if the world their children were growing up in, would be a safer, more peaceful and happier place.

Sam had felt during his time as a POW that he would like to do something if he got back. Something to stop such a war from happening again. He was only one person of course, but he felt his life needed that purpose.

During his time in the army, he met many people in a whole range of different circumstances. Some had acted kindly, unselfishly and even at times heroically to the circumstances they faced. And some of these were grim indeed. Some, on the other hand, had acted cruelly and often had taken advantage of situations to inflict pain and duress when they had no need to, even in difficult dilemmas, when they might have to make life-and-death choices.

These people were not necessarily on the Allies' side. In fact, he had found that people would if they could, do the best for themselves and others, no matter which nation, background or 'side' they were on. Nationalist conflicts were caused by governments and leaders. He believed no one wanted wars with the ravages and pain they created. If people really found the time to understand each other he believed most conflict could be avoided. These thoughts unsettled him. Christine and he discussed these issues well when the demands of parenthood allowed them to, and both were on the same page.

The problem was what to do and how to do it. As often happens in these situations, serendipitous opportunities arise to satisfy these needs.

Neil, one of Sam's colleagues, mentioned to him that their local MP was holding an open meeting in a local hall to discuss local issues. He said he had been to one of these before and found unexpectedly that it had been really interesting. He urged Sam to come along to this meeting as they had both often discussed the issues that preyed on Sam's mind. Sam was reluctant at first. Life was busy enough with his job and being a parent.

"I'll give it some thought, Neil," he said. "Politics is not really my thing. It seems to me it's more 'hot air' than concrete progress. I'll have a chat with Christine tonight and see what she thinks"

"I see under the wife's thumb, eh. Need to get her permission, do you?" he laughed, and Sam chuckled in response.

That night, he did find time to talk to Christine about it. She was surprisingly enthusiastic, especially as she wouldn't be able to go as someone had to look after the kids.

"I know you've said many times politics is not your thing. You've often condemned politicians as the ones who start wars. But you have this need inside you to do more. I can see it and feel it. So go and explore. It might confirm your doubts, but you never know, do you?"

The meeting was the following Friday, and Sam had made up his mind to go. It was held in a workmen's club in Cardiff. He travelled by bus the five miles there, and as he had not been that way for a while, he was amazed at the progress made in renovating and rebuilding. Cardiff had got off lightly relatively from the bombing, but even so, the damage had been considerable. It also made him reflect on the damage that had been done to many, many cities in Europe. It was easy to say as they started the war, they deserved

177

what had happened. It was not as simple as that, though. Unless nations pulled together and helped each other recover, then the struggle for survival would likely bring further conflict in the future.

He was greeted on his arrival and directed to where to sit. The room looked like it would hold a couple of hundred and was filling up quite quickly. People were chatty and friendly, as he had found many people in the Welsh capital to be.

Soon, the candidate appeared on the stage accompanied by two others who introduced themselves as the local chairman and the candidate's agent. Then, after a short introduction, the candidate stood up and made his speech.

Sam became fully engrossed in most of what was being said. The plans to rebuild Britain and to provide free health to all, he knew were exactly what was needed.

After the speech, he made his way to the local chairman and chatted enthusiastically with him about the ideas that had been presented and asked how he could become involved in helping.

As he walked homeward that evening, he knew he had to get involved. He had seen what happened when people's wishes were ignored and when people slept, while power-hungry leaders took over. He wanted to help, and now he could see how.

This could be part of his future. A chance to fix things and make a difference. And he knew Christine would be enthusiastic, too.

A new beginning. Perhaps some of the experiences they both had had could be worth it, if they both could make a difference, however small it may be. How could they possibly retreat to ordinary lives after all they had been through, and, with a chance to make a better world for their children?

Postscript

All the incidents in this story are based on real people and real events.

Although, many people suffered terribly because of the war, what happened after the war shows what can happen when we pull together.

As the war-torn nations of Europe faced famine and economic crisis in the wake of World War II, the United States proposed to rebuild the continent in the interest of political stability and a healthy world economy. The Marshall Plan was a success. By 1950, the participating countries had returned to, or exceeded, their pre-war production levels.

Printed in Great Britain
by Amazon

51210187R00106